What on earth can grow in rocky

Today's world is brimming with promise. But contradictions abound. Everywhere people are crying out for an end to mindless violence and for the renewing of a sterile culture, for reconciliation, compassion, equality. We search for the soil in which such qualities can take root.

Too easily we assume that nothing will grow anyway. Yet seeds sprout in the most unlikely places. And creative dialogue can take place between the bitterest enemies.

Can something vital come from ruin, war and suffering?

A deadlocked situation, large or small, can shift when one or two people decide to take risks – to cross the no-man's-land, to listen to enemies and opponents, to expose their own search for a different approach.

The trouble is that human nature is so capable of cruelty, arrogance, exploitation and dishonesty.

But in every human heart there is also the ability to cherish, to sacrifice, to reach for what is creative and nourishing. We do not have to submit to the worst in the world or in ourselves. The choices are wider, deeper and simpler than we think.

Dresden

Coventry

Beirut

Saigon

*I*n 1945, as World War II drew to its end, a small group of Swiss struggled with a challenging fact. Their country had escaped the devastation. But the hatreds unleashed around them threatened to make it happen all over again.

Could a healing and reconciling spirit take deep enough root to prevent history repeating itself, they asked themselves? Should it even grow from Swiss soil?

El Salvador   Afghanistan

Bosnia

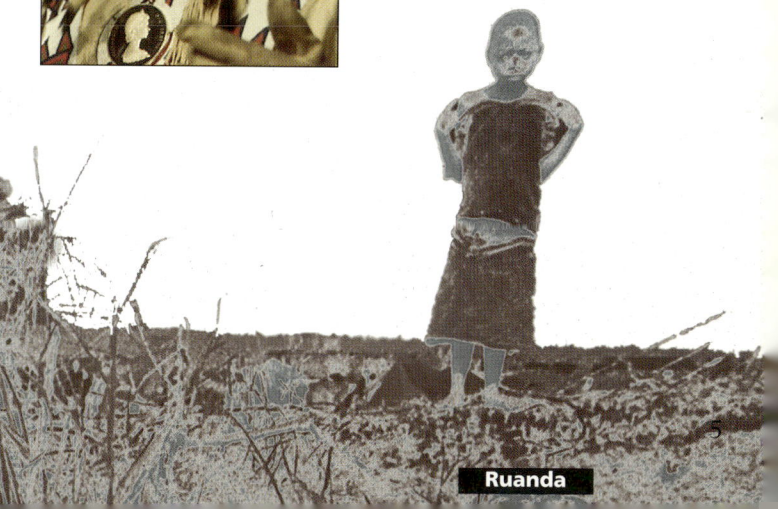

Ruanda

Where could war-weary nations come together?

At Interlaken, less than a year after the end of the war, these Swiss hosted a meeting of 180 people from 12 European nations. Many of them had not seen each other since they had last met, seven and a half years earlier, in that same town. In September 1938, with war threatening, they had gathered in Interlaken for the first 'world assembly for moral re-armament'.

This informal movement – MRA as it became known – had sprung from the interaction between Oxford University students and an American Lutheran pastor named Frank Buchman. Buchman was not interested in starting yet another organisation. He saw the need for something far more organic – a wave of change in society set in motion by individuals putting right where they themselves were wrong, rather than hurling accusations at others. 'God has a plan for the world,' he would say, 'and you have a part in it.'

In a world clogged by the Depression and appalled by the rise of Hitler and Stalin, the idea that real change has to start with oneself had an earthy practicality. As the European crisis intensified, large gatherings of people who wanted to try this approach took place in several countries – Britain, the Netherlands, Scandinavia and Switzerland, for instance. Following that first Interlaken assembly, Buchman was given a lunch at the League of Nations in Geneva on September 15, 1938, the very day British Prime Minister

Chamberlain flew to Berchtesgaden to see Hitler in a futile search for 'peace in our time'. Buchman told diplomats from 53 countries present, 'We need to call into being a whole new philosophy of living – that quality of life that is above party, above class, above faction, above nations – people unitedly under God's control.' His host at the lunch was C J Hambro, a Norwegian Member of Parliament who was to become the last President of the League of Nations. Speaking about Buchman and his colleagues, Hambro said, 'In this hour of grave apprehension and fear it is of vital importance to meet hope and faith and strength. Where we have failed in changing politics, they have succeeded in changing lives.'

Among the Swiss responsible for the Interlaken gatherings was Philippe Mottu. In 1944 Mottu, by then a diplomat in his 30s, and his wife Hélène were invited by Frank Buchman to join him in America. During the war Mottu had come across senior Germans who were profoundly opposed to Hitler. One of them, the diplomat Adam von Trott, asked Mottu to take to America a list of those who would form a new German government if the planned coup against Hitler succeeded. The failure of the coup and von Trott's execution were shattering blows for Mottu. They reinforced his conviction that something extraordinary would be needed if a new Europe was to be born.

Buchman believed that God can give ideas to people who are willing to search for them objectively and without conditions. In one such time of quiet reflection as early as 1942, Mottu had thought of a huge hotel above Lake Geneva in a village called Caux. And at Interlaken in 1946, he was keen to explore its possibilities.

'Where we have failed in changing politics, they have succeeded in changing lives.'

Carl Hambro, Buchman's host at the League of Nations

When it opened on July 7, 1902, the Caux-Palace was the biggest and most luxurious hotel in Switzerland. Among the guests in its heyday were John D Rockefeller, the Maharajah of Baroda (whose drawing-room, specially furnished in citron-wood, still exists), the violinist Ysaye and other great stars of music, opera and the stage, the thriller-writer Edgar

In a huge old hotel above Lake Geneva

The Maharajah of Baroda, the violinist Ysaye, thriller-writer Edgar Wallace and Prince Ibn Saud of Saudi Arabia were among its guests...

Wallace, and Prince Ibn Saud, later to become King of Saudi Arabia. Olympic skating champions trained at Caux; world federations of bobsleigh, tobogganing and ice hockey were founded there; and the run from the mountains above, the *piste du diable*, gained a reputation as one of the toughest tests available for the new sport of skiing.

During World War I the Palace was empty for five years and lost a million francs. It reopened but its facilities had deteriorated and it was not till 1929 that its owners found a further million francs to refurbish it. Too late, because the Depression struck, and then World War II. In May 1944 the building was reopened to house British and American prisoners of war who had escaped from Italy; and from October 1944 to July 1945, Italian refugees and Jewish exiles from Hungary were crammed six to eight in a room.

built in an age of luxury and elegance

7

It was derelict... and for sale, not for rent

It was an awesome sum ...but also a bargain

One day in March 1946, Philippe and Hélène Mottu drove to Caux to see whether they could rent the hotel for the summer. The caretaker told them that it was about to be sold by the Banque Populaire Suisse to a French company who would rip all the fittings out of it and leave an empty shell on the mountainside. An hour later, without waiting to look over the building, Mottu was with the manager of the bank's Montreux branch. He discovered that two companies were bidding for the Palace.

So renting was out of the question: if they wanted the place they would have to buy it. The bank recognised that it would be better for the region if the building was to remain intact; and on 6 May, the day on which the other groups had asked for an answer, the bank decided to suspend negotiations with them. On the 25th Mottu and Robert Hahnloser signed a contract to buy the hotel, at a lower price than the demolishers had offered: SFr 1,050,000 – 100,000 immediately, 450,000 by 1 July and the rest by year's end.

It was an awesome sum. But also a bargain. The Palace Hotel had originally cost six million francs to build. At 1946 exchange rates, they were being offered it for £130,000, or US$524,000. So where would this money come from?

All the participants in the decision look back on this

Peyer, Mottu and Hahnloser: where would the money come from?

phase with awe. One of them was able to write the first cheque for SFr100,000: but it was clear that the whole sum would be raised only from the sacrifice of many people. Ninety-five families took part in raising the SFr 450,000 needed by 1 July. One family which was planning to build a new house stayed in their old one and gave the money instead. Holiday houses, jewellery and other precious possessions were sold. The deadlines were met. The Mottus' cook, Trudi Trüssel, had the surprising thought that she should give two months' wages. Obeying it was the start of a belief that perhaps God existed and had something for her to do. She volunteered to cook at Caux, and did so for many years until the work became too much. She then became custodian of the mail room, and still looks after a stream of people who appear every morning at her window.

Dedicated to meticulous Swiss standards

Early in the negotiations, the most responsible of the Swiss group – among them the Mottus, engineers Robert Hahnloser and Erich Peyer and their wives – had visited Caux. They were excited by the scope of the building but devastated by the condition in which they found it. The kitchen was 'like a coal mine'. Meals for the refugees had been cooked on army field kitchens, designed for use in the open air. Its floor had to be dug up and the whole place disinfected. Floors and furniture had been chopped up for firewood and lift-wells filled with rubbish. The women, dedicated to meticulous Swiss standards, felt particularly shattered and some were in tears. This was what they were about to buy! And if they did, they would need to have it ready for a conference of more than 500 people in eight or nine weeks.

They sat in the little café at the Caux railway station, with glasses of scalding coffee, and began to talk it out. After a while, conversation was inadequate. If ever they needed the wisdom of the Almighty! Was God really putting this task before them? Dorli Hahnloser, Robert's wife, broke the silence. '"Streams of living water will flow",' she said. What they faced took on an entirely new shape.

A locksmith repaired over 800 locks

Trudi Trüssel, one of the first to contribute: and now in charge of the mail room

Could it be ready for 500 people in nine weeks?

More than a hundred Swiss took leave from their jobs, and dozens came from other parts of Europe, to clean every room and corridor, to wash every sheet and blanket, to dig, paint, scrub, saw and hammer.

Urgent work was needed on the door locks. The craftsman head of a small family firm, pondering how to help prepare 'Mountain House' (as the Caux-Palace had been renamed), decided to be responsible for metalwork repairs, starting with the locks. He asked his 79-year-old locksmith father and an apprentice to tackle the job, and in the next five weeks they checked and repaired over 800 locks.

The visit led to a stirring reconciliation between the businessman and his father, who had felt bitter at having to hand over the firm. The businessman went on to do many other jobs in Caux without charge. There are a host of such stories.

A British couple, who came to help prepare the hotel and stayed on for seven years, tell of a Swiss textile manufacturer who called a meeting in Zurich of others in his trade. Most of them contributed furnishings, one giving 2,000 bed sheets.

On 9 July eight cooks from five nations – who had to draw each other pictures of the vegetables because they had no common language – made the first meal for 150 people. And by month's end, as scheduled, the first major assembly was in full swing.

A volunteer stage crew prepared for the first productions in the Caux theatre

The kitchen was 'like a coal mine'. Its floor had to be dug up and the whole place disinfected.

The first meals cooked by an international team of cooks... and (*right*) crowds assemble for the opening conference

Then & Now

It was an enormous gamble. If they had been trying, with good Swiss caution, to make a small contribution to post-war Europe, they should have kept looking for a place to rent. In the semi-derelict building they had just bought with so many people's savings, could they get through the summer of 1946? And what about 1947, 48, 49...? Would the volunteers come back?

They did. And are still coming. Some for the first time, some for the fiftieth. The running and financing of this complex has been a saga in itself. The diverse, ever-evolving collection of people who have done it are a global community in microcosm – teenagers to octogenarians, high-profile public figures and unknown individuals, from practically every ethnic and philosophic background conceivable.

When we were first asked to create this account of Caux, we thought it must be a joke. We live on the southern edge of Australia, about as far from Switzerland as you can get. But we have known of Caux since 1950, and it has given us a tantalising glimpse of creative options for the world. So we accepted the assignment. It's been harder than we expected to capture hundreds of individual experiences and their accumulated effect. Any shortcomings are nobody's fault but ours.

Today's future looks very different from that of 1946. Technology shrinks distances, and communication is becoming unbelievably cheap and easy, for some at least. So understanding and justice should be more possible than ever. But then so are self-interest, division and criminal manipulation.

Excellence could be normal, but we are just as likely to choose the second- or tenth-best. Witness the scars of today's ethnic and racial flashpoints. The potential of what goes on at Caux is as great as in those first stark post-war years. Many groups are working at bringing the world together, and Caux's most valuable days may lie ahead.

Back then, the pioneers had a simple aim: a new society through a change in people. They were realistic enough to know that this was beyond human organisation, and believed that the Spirit of God can transform any situation if people search for how it might happen.

In its first half century the Caux community has experienced times of inspiration and times of struggle; moments of great clarity and periods of searching. It has been a learning experience, because this one has had the human failings of any community. Yet the basic call to which the founders of Caux responded is still what keeps it going and growing. And the seeds of hope, germinating through the response of individuals and sprouting in green shoots of initiative, have time and again made the gamble worthwhile.

So there's a story to be heard. Back to 1946, and a battered Europe...

Mike Brown   John Williams

Green shoots among Europe's ruins

The first Assembly opened in July 1946 in the renovated 'Mountain House'. On his arrival a few days earlier, Frank Buchman (fourth from right, with Philippe Mottu and British journalist Peter Howard) had turned to Mottu and asked after the five Germans he had been told were somewhere in the house. He added, 'You will never rebuild Europe without the Germans.'

His comment spread rapidly through the house. It was barely a year since the end of the war. 'The effect was stunning. Shock, outrage, anger showed on many faces. Supper that night was a subdued meal and many were strangely silent,' said one of many war-veterans there.

Suddenly they realised they might soon actually be meeting people who had been their enemies for nearly six years...

11

Between 1946 and 1950 a total of 3,113 Germans were in Caux – 'a fair proportion of the entire (West) German elite', to quote a recent study of peacemaking by the Center for Strategic and International Studies, Washington, DC. They included 85 MPs, 400 trade unionists, 210 industrialists, 160 media people.

There they met their opposite numbers from Europe and other continents: 1,983 French citizens, for instance, including 200 trade unionists and 207 industrialists.

But back in 1946, the question was how the potential leaders of a new Germany could discover that Caux even existed, let alone get there. There was an almost total ban on travel. The Allied occupation authorities, keen to reinforce democratic principles, helped. And one morning in June 1947, 150 from many parts of Germany arrived together. All told, 5,000 people from 50 countries went to Caux that second summer. The Germans were greeted by a French chorus singing a welcome song in German.

Could those who had fought each other now face each other?

French socialist Irène Laure

'I fully expected to hear people say, "What are these criminals doing here?",' said Peter Petersen, a Hitler Youth member from the age of seven. Petersen had been wounded in the final German retreat and thrown into a British prison. 'We were past masters at defending ourselves,' he added, 'but here the doors were wide open for us.'

A week later, he and his friends were 'flabbergasted' to hear Irène Laure, a member of the Executive of the French Socialist Party, say, 'I hated Germany so much that I would have liked to see it erased from the map of Europe. But I have seen here that my hatred was wrong. I would like to ask all the Germans present to forgive me.'

'For several nights,' Petersen recalls, 'I could not sleep. My whole past was in revolt against the courage of this woman. I suddenly realised that there were things for which we, as individuals and as a nation, could never

'My whole past was in revolt... There were things for which we could never make restitution.'
Peter Petersen

make restitution. Yet we knew, my friends and I, that she had shown us the only way open to Germany. The basis of a new Europe would have to be forgiveness.'

After several days the young Germans 'told her how ashamed we were for all the things she and her people had had to suffer through our fault'.

'What kind of unity do you want?'

Irène Laure had vigorously resisted the very idea of going to Caux. Between the wars she had tried to help create Franco-German friendship in small ways like having German children to stay for holidays. But when the Panzer divisions rolled into France she risked her life nightly with the Underground. Her son Louis had been tortured. 'They tried everything. He never talked. But the state we found him in! He was a wreck,' she said.

When she finally arrived at Caux, with two of her five children who badly needed proper food, she found Germans there. 'Their presence was unendurable,' she said later, and she was on the point of leaving when in one of the long corridors she happened to meet Frank Buchman. 'Madame Laure,' he said, 'you're a socialist. How can you expect to rebuild Europe if you reject the German people? What kind of unity do you want for Europe?'

'If he had pitied me or sympathised with me,' she said later, 'I'd have left.' Instead she went back to her room and agonised over the question for many hours. Then she agreed to have lunch with a German woman. The meal began in silence until, perspiration breaking out on her forehead, Irène Laure poured out all she had lived through. Then she looked at the German for the first time and said, 'I'm telling you all this, Madame, because I want to be free of this hate.'

The German was the widow of Adam von Trott, the diplomat involved in the plot against Hitler. She too was silent, and then described her own suffering in prison when her husband was hanged and their children put in an orphanage under false names. 'Now I have found them again, and am bringing them up as best I can. I realise that we did not resist enough, or in time. Because of this you have suffered terribly. Please forgive us.'

Mme Laure surprised herself by suggesting they pray together. 'Oh God,' she said, 'free me from my hate so we can build a better world for our children.'

The next day she said the sentences which had such an effect on Peter Petersen. 'What I learnt at Caux,' she said later, 'was how to forgive. That is a huge thing, because one can die of hatred. Hatred is an incredibly strong force. Unity is also a force. Isn't it a woman's role, a mother's role, to maintain the links?'

In 1948, 260 people left Caux to tour five German cities with a revue, *The Good Road*, playing to packed audiences, and with a photographic exhibition

...in Caux, and also in Germany?

For those risking leadership in a country which, as a Berlin journalist said, had been 'branded with darkness, resignation, bitterness and confusion', it was extremely therapeutic to be able to talk with those who had been traumatised on the other side. It also helped that the conference theme was a search for where change might be needed in everyone. So the Germans were not especially on the spot. And there was work for everyone to do. They speedily got to know people from other places as they fried potatoes for a thousand or struggled with an ancient dishwashing machine.

But this was not just mingling in a spirit of easy goodwill. Reinhold Maier, Minister-President of Württemberg-Baden, saw a play in the Caux theatre about Norwegian resistance hero Frederik Ramm. Returning to his room, he threw himself on his bed, 'completely shattered' at what Germany had done. 'It was a presentation without hatred or complaint, and therefore could hardly have been more powerful in its effect,' he wrote afterwards.

'We've often tried to make democracy a reality,' said one political leader, 'but never succeeded': this phase was Germany's 'last chance'. The Germans put their heads together and came up with a plan for presenting what they had discovered to their country.

Firstly they invited Mme Laure and her husband Victor to Germany. In 11 weeks, the Laures addressed 200 meetings, including 10 of the 11 state parliaments.

Then the Germans created a pamphlet, *Es muss alles anders werden* (*Everything's got to be different*). The publishing committee was headed up by the President of the Bavarian Parliament, and eventually, thanks to gifts of paper from Sweden and America, a million and a quarter copies were published and distributed, 400,000 of them in the Russian Zone.

In Caux they had seen a musical revue called *The Good Road* which dramatised people's efforts to make democracy work, with sketches from farm, factory and home and historical scenes. In October 1948 they invited it to tour five German cities, and in 15 days it was performed to packed audiences 16 times.

Allied ex-servicemen gave their war gratuities towards the tour's financial needs and an American doctor cashed his insurance policies and gave $40,000. Leading the invitation committee were Minister-President Karl Arnold of North-Rhine Westphalia and his cabinet, and two other Minister-Presidents.

So great was the response that Karl Arnold's government asked urgently for a similar action to continue. His state included the Ruhr, home of 80 per cent of German heavy industry. And as his Minister of Labour, August Halbfell, said, 'On every lip is whether the ideas of Washington or Moscow will dominate this region.' Halbfell wanted neither. But which way could they find that would put other countries' fears at rest?

In 1948 it became clear that the world was facing a long Cold War and every chance of a short but cataclysmic hot one...

The US, through the Marshall Plan, gave Europe $12 billion worth of goods and services with which to rebuild. The Russians blockaded Berlin, which was only saved by the Airlift from being swallowed up, as so much of Eastern Europe had been. A Cominform document in January predicted that the Ruhr would be a centre of 'mass struggle in Germany', and added, 'The coming winter will be the decisive period in the history of the German working class.'

As the Cold War set in, new approaches began to emerge

Ruhr miners Kurowski (left) and Bladeck: 'Class war and its tactics are suicide'

Such a challenge could never be met with mere anti-Communism. So what would be adequate? This question stretched imaginations among the Caux fraternity, those from Germany and everywhere else. The head of the German Coal Board, Dr Heinrich Kost, asked Frank Buchman, ' What do we do now? When Hitler was around, he told us what to do. If the Russians come, they will tell us what to do. What do you say we should do?' Buchman replied, 'I can't tell you what to do, nor would it be right for me to do so. But I can tell you how to find out for yourself.' Kost decided to search his own heart and attitudes for anything God might be asking of him.

In response to Halbfell's request, another play, *The Forgotten Factor*, was produced with a German cast. The story of a strike which involved two families, the boss's and the trade union leader's, it was seen in the next two years by 120,000 people, and created a ferment about how justice and social change could be achieved. Scores of people from the area went to Caux to talk further, a number of them veteran Communists who had only sur-

vived Hitler's ideology by becoming more fiercely committed to Marxism. They would invite the international visitors into their homes and clubs for conversations that would continue for four or five very solid hours, buttressed by massive quotes from Marx and Lenin.

Kost had invited the play to the mines in the town of Moers, where it was seen by hundreds of Communists including Max Bladeck, Chairman of the Works Councils in the five mines, and Paul Kurowski, who was responsible for training party functionaries for the area. Their initial position was that Western Europe was preparing a new world war because 'every single capitalist is a fascist at heart', and 'there is no ideology above class'. But at Caux Bladeck was to say that he had discovered there an ideology 'that does not set one man against another but shows how a man may make enemies into friends'. Kurowski said: 'I have sung the *Internationale* for 26 years with all my heart, but here for the first time I have seen it lived.' He concluded: 'The basic theories of Marxism are outmoded. Its thought system does not reckon with the important fact that human nature can be changed. Class war

and its tactics are suicide, for it must of necessity end in world-wide war between two opposing camps and lead to total destruction.'

They were joined by another activist, Willi Benedens, who had lost both legs in the war. He concluded: 'In Caux I found the thing I had been fighting for through the years – a classless society.' When they got back to the Ruhr, they were carpeted at Communist headquarters. The Party should get to know 'Moral Re-Armament's world-revolutionising idea', they argued, for the sake of its own development. But they were expelled, and Hugo Paul, Chairman of the North-Rhine Westphalia Executive, in an article in the Dusseldorf Communist paper headed 'Unmoral Disarmament' said that all comrades who associated with them would also be thrown out.

Stoffmehl, a veteran of 40 years in the Communist Party, pounded the table and said 'This is not right! Are they afraid of Caux?'

Many Communists were distressed by this ruling. Hermann Stoffmehl, a Party veteran who was Town Clerk in Alten-Essen, pounded the table and said, 'This is not right! Are they afraid of Caux?'

The struggle came to a head at a conference chaired by the Vice-Chairman of the whole West German Communist Party, where Hugo Paul moved

The German Coal Board and miners' leaders from 150 pits at a conference in Essen, to hear speakers from Caux

Mining Company, with 27,000 workers one of the region's largest employers, visited Caux in 1949, for what he expected would be a mountain-climbing holiday. When he got back Dütting decided to put all his financial cards on the table with his workers 'in such a way that we no longer had the slightest thing to hide. The result was an extraordinary growth in trust between workforce and management.' He began by asking the works councillors to help him put straight a wrong decision he had made. At Caux in 1950, his works council chairman, Paul Dikus, called Dütting's action 'something entirely new. And look at all the other things that have happened – all the houses that are being built, all the new social amenities for the workers.'

West Germany's Federal Chancellor, Konrad Adenauer, had asked Böckler if the trade unions would agree to give up the idea of public ownership and instead accept *Mitbestimmung* or co-determination, whereby the workers would have equal representation on the boards of large public companies. Ruhr barons, Communists and former Nazis were all against it. Dikus and Dütting saw it as part of the new process. As Dütting said, 'On the basis of the same ideology we understand each other better and better.' Böckler and his colleagues agreed to this groundbreaking idea, which did a lot to open the way for Germany's 'economic miracle'. The co-determination law was passed in two stages in May 1951 and October 1952.

Every refugee an asset

The Caux community never sought to intervene in the political process of any country, but they did hope to raise expectations of what the 'art of the possible' could attempt. The Reconstruction Minister for North-Rhine Westphalia, Dr Otto Schmidt, said at Caux in 1951, 'We cannot evaluate in detail what it means that since 1947 thousands of people in public life have been to Caux.' He added that Buchman's phrase, 'When everyone cares enough and everyone shares enough, everyone has enough', had provided a key thought.

Dr Hans Lukaschek, West German Minister of Refugees at that time, said that his visits to Caux had encouraged him to look on every refugee from the East not as another mouth to feed but as an asset for the rebuilding of Germany. He and his successor, who had also been at Caux frequently, created a 'law of equalization of burdens', by which those with capital or property paid a special once-only tax over 20 years amounting to half their wealth after a tax-free minimum, so that refugees could have regular payments as well as some compensation.

Changed perspectives often began with personal encounters, such as that which developed there in 1949 between Hans Böckler and the President of the French Employers' Federation, Georges Villiers, who was representing French statesman Robert Schuman. Over a meal, Böckler said, 'We ought to be enemies on two counts – I am German, you are French. You are the head of the employers, I'm a trade union leader.' Villiers replied, 'There's a third count. Your countrymen condemned me to death. I was in a political concentration camp. I saw most of my comrades die around me. But that is all past. We must forget it. And personally, I would like to shake your hand.' Such reconciliations were building blocks in the creation of modern Europe.

Union leader Dikus and manager Dütting: 'All the financial cards on the table'

that no Party member could go to Caux and that every Communist was duty bound to combat MRA. In reply Stoffmehl's resolution stated: 'We functionaries of the German Communist Party here assembled are unanimous in accepting the aim of Moral Re-Armament as a basis for discussion.' Stoffmehl lost the vote by a whisker, 400 to 407, and in the coming years hundreds of Communists left the Party. Bladeck and others won increased majorities in works council elections and Communist representation dropped in two years from 72 to 25 per cent.

When the structure of society changes

One of the architects of the new Germany was the President of the Trade Union Federation, Dr Hans Böckler. He sat at the back of a meeting of industrialists called by Dr Kost to hear from MRA speakers, and said he was impressed that the same challenges were given to industrialists as to workers' leaders. Visiting Caux he said: 'If men are to be free from the old and the out-moded, it can happen only as they set themselves new goals and place humanity and moral values in the forefront. When men change, the structure of society changes, and when the structure of society changes, men change. Both go together and both are necessary.'

Hans Dütting, Director of the Gelsenkirchen Coal

'An invisible but effective part in bridging the differences

It is easy to forget, now that we have such a strong European Union, how daring it was in the late 1940s even to conceive the first step towards this, the Schuman Plan, through which former enemies combined their resources to make future war impossible.

At the beginning of 1950 it seemed as if the Plan might fail. Jean Monnet, who had drafted it, said to Schuman at a frigid meeting that January in Bonn, 'We are on the brink of making the same mistake as in 1919.' It was finally signed in April 1951, and in June, Chancellor Adenauer wrote to Frank Buchman, 'In recent months we have seen the conclusion, after some difficult negotiations, of important international agreements. Here Moral Re-Armament has played an invisible but effective part in bridging differences of opinion between negotiating parties, and has kept before them the object of peaceful agreement in the search for the common good.'

Adenauer and Schuman both visited Caux, Adenauer in 1947 and Schuman in 1953. In October 1949, shortly before the negotiations reached their crucial stage, Schuman and Buchman had dinner together. Schuman said he was unsure whom to trust in the new Germany, and Buchman gave him a list of 'some excellent men' who had been in Caux.

In February 1950, Schuman wrote the foreword to the French edition of Buchman's speeches. He identified three aspects of Buchman's program based in Caux: to create 'a moral climate in which true brotherly unity can flourish'; to understand what was needed 'by bringing people together' and 'to provide teams of trained people, apostles of reconciliation and builders of a new world'. This, he wrote, was 'the beginning of a far-reaching transformation of society in which the first steps have already been made'.

The French Government, recognising Buchman's 'contribution to better understanding between France and Germany', made him a Chevalier of the Legion of Honour in 1950. Two years later, the German Government awarded him the Grand Cross of the Order of Merit for 'his significant work for peace and understanding between nations'.

When Frank Buchman died in 1961 the German Government's official *Bulletin* wrote that through Caux 'he brought Germany back into the circle of civilised nations... Caux became one of the great moral forces to which we owe our new standing in the world... The foundations of the understanding between Germany and France were laid by the first meetings between Germans and French at Caux.'

'The foundations of the understanding between Germany and France were laid by those first meetings at Caux.'

German Chancellor Adenauer: 'The conclusion of some difficult negotiations'

Foreign Minister Schuman (*left*) with Buchman in Caux, 1953: 'The beginning of a far-reaching transformation...'

Then & Now
One man's experience

That Leif Hovelsen even agreed to go to Germany was remarkable. As a 19-year-old student in Oslo, he had been pulled from his bed by the Gestapo in the middle of the night, betrayed by a fellow member of the Resistance. His Gestapo interrogator told him he was on the list for execution. He was due to go by boat to a Nazi liquidation camp in Germany, but he and three others were left behind. Ten others close to him were shot.

In solitary confinement, Hovelsen had a profound experience of God's presence which convinced him that, whatever happened, God had a purpose for his life. This was reinforced by an experience right after the war. He and others were on guard duty over some Germans when his former camp commandant and special security officers were brought in. One of them 'had inflicted punishment drills on one of my friends so ruthlessly that my friend died of a heart attack.'

Gleefully they put their former captors through the same drills. One asked for water and Hovelsen threw a bucket of it over him. This made him very popular, but he felt uncomfortable. 'I despised myself. I wanted to fight for right and justice, but this was lust for revenge. In my own nature there was the root of the same evil of which I was accusing National Socialism and the

... in the search for the common good'

As the new Europe began to take shape, Caux was year by year a meeting place of people and ideas.

On one of several visits, Jean Rey, President of the EEC Commission from 1967 to 1970, stressed that the European Community has 'a spiritual rather than an economic base. Its basis is reconciliation and an end to centuries of the monstrous stupidity of killing each other... If ever we lose our sense of destiny for Europe, this is one place, Caux, where we are reminded of it.'

Europe's stability is still gravely threatened by its minorities in conflict. As Dr Karl Mitterdorfer, President of the Federative Union of European Nationalities, said at Caux in 1992: 'Frontiers are the scars of history, particularly when they have been drawn unfairly. These wounds represent potential danger if we fail to transform frontier areas into meeting places. We will not be able to achieve this unless we suppress in our hearts the barriers of hatred, selfishness and bitterness. One learns how to do that at Caux.'

Mitterdorfer was speaking from experience of a minority problem that had divided Italy and Austria for 45 years. During World War I the Allies secretly promised South Tyrol, a province of the Austro-Hungarian Empire, to Italy if she would fight against Germany. 200,000 German-speaking people suddenly found themselves Italian. Mussolini banished the German language and culture. By 1959 bombs were being thrown.

In 1969, a group from both sides including Mitterdorfer visited Caux. Dr Silvius Magnago, Governor of South Tyrol, said to an opponent, 'Next time we meet we shall not glare at each other but meet in friendship because of our experiences here.'

Agreement on South Tyrol was being frustrated at the time by a threatened split in the main political party. Mitterdorfer, as leader of one of these groups, began seeking God's direction, and had the insistent thought that he should talk with the leader of the other group. He did not find this easy, 'for there is a principle that a politician should never admit he has done anything wrong. But after some inner struggle and many postponements, I apologised for the many wrong things between us. The result was remarkable. My relationship with this opponent became quite different. This affected our relationship with politicians and parties outside our ranks.'

The agreement reached that year and finally ratified in 1992 'does not mean all our problems are solved,' said Mitterdorfer. 'But it should guarantee the survival of our culture and language.'

'Frontiers are the wounds of history, particularly when they have been drawn unfairly.'

Germans.' After much thought he summoned the Gestapo agent who had treated him worst and forgave him. When the man was put on trial, Hovelsen would not give evidence. The agent was later condemned and executed on the evidence of others.

Within three years Hovelsen had abandoned his university studies and joined some 20 others from several countries who had put themselves at the disposal of the Germans who had been in Caux. It was unpaid work, but pivotal in the interchange between Germany and Caux. For seven years they moved with their suitcases from house to house as invited. Hovelsen later wrote, 'What we were living for was something that went far deeper than any political programme. In sharing the cares and joys, the ups and downs of our friends, we became part of the life that was stirring in the Ruhr... It was a battle to set men free, a battle to find out the reasons for our hate and jealousy, the reasons why we are at the mercy of our desires.'

As the Cold War thawed, Hovelsen became a friend of many dissidents such as Andrei Sakharov and Milovan Djilas. In recent years he has repeatedly been in Moscow, introducing many Russians to Caux. One of them, a leading intellectual, told him Russia needs 'a moral and spiritual renaissance that can give our freedom a deeper content and the democratic process a stable framework.' Hovelsen comments: 'We need that in the West as well. We must reach out to the peoples of Eastern Europe, whose experience of fundamental human rights is practically nil. Could we together pioneer a deeper conception of what freedom with responsibility and care means?'

(Left) President of the EEC Commission Jean Rey at Caux

(right) Italian Member of the European Parliament Giovanni Bersani with ANC spokesmen Henry Fazzie **(right)** and Ike Maphoto

(below) Karl Mitterdorfer, president of the Federative Union of European Nationalities, with Xhafer Shatri, director of the Kosovo information bureau in Geneva

Values for democracy, a priority for both East and West

The fall of the Berlin Wall was one of the world's great turning points this century. But would the return of democratic processes to Central and Eastern Europe be enough? Frank Buchman's question to Irène Laure, 'What kind of Europe do you want to build?' is as valid as ever. Can democracies on both sides of the former Curtain be free of corruption and ethnic violence – a source, indeed, of genuine equality and brotherhood? And proof against future dictators? These, surely, are questions for all of us, wherever we live.

Before the Wall fell, Vienna's Cardinal Franz König foresaw what would be needed. In 1986, at the 40th anniversary celebrations of the Caux complex, he pointed out that it was Frank Buchman 'who had had the courage to tell the French, Americans and British that without the Germans a new Europe could not be built', and asked, 'Is it not now a further task for Moral Re-Armament to initiate a common thought process that will start a dialogue between East and West, despite all the differences in mentality?'

Since then hundreds of people from all these countries have made their way to Caux, and have contributed greatly to its processes. 'At last all the members of the European family are at home together,' said one member of the Caux community who had made many trips to the former Soviet empire. 'Those from the East,' he added, deeply moved, 'find here people from the West ready to listen and understand.'

In Caux in 1992, Yuri Senokosov, a Russian philosopher, convened a four-day international seminar on 'the moral lessons of Soviet history – the experience of opposition to evil'. This drew leading academics not only from Russia, but also from Poland, Ukraine, Germany, France, Switzerland, Austria, Italy, Britain and the USA. Such events have been well-reported in the East European press.

One participant, the Russian historian and philosopher Grigory Pomerants, described his experience of Caux in November 1994 in *Novoye Vremya*, and recorded how much he had learned from Leif Hovelsen's decision to forgive his Nazi torturers. In a further article in *Literaturnaya Gazeta*, Prof Pomerants called for 'readiness of the heart for dialogue, readiness to listen to the spirit that is deeper than words, and to feel as one's greater body not only one's own people but foreign peoples, not only people but everything that lives. Moral rearmament is needed both by the frustrated terrorist and by the peaceful, law-abiding citizen who has long since forgotten what the soul is. I believe in the possibility of a world civilisation where the European principle of a dialogue of nations... is supplemented by a dialogue of the great coalitions of culture, a dialogue of approaches to the one God. But for the spirit to prevail, a great renewal is necessary. In each of us there is a struggle between the spirit of love and the spirit of strife and destruction. The question of the future is always open.'

Meetings at Caux between East and West have led to a great variety of visits back and forth – MPs from the Ukraine and Poland investigating Western democracy; people from the nations around the Baltic sea seeking reconciliation and regional cooperation; stage plays and musical and artistic forums; and many programs for students. Under the title *Foundations for Freedom*, a series of international courses have begun annually at the

Austria's Cardinal König: start a dialogue 'between East and West, despite all the differences'

'Moral rearmament is needed both by the frustrated terrorist and by the peaceful, law-abiding citizen who has long since forgotten what the soul is.'

Russian writer and philosopher Professor Grigory Pomerants (left)

MRA centre in England, and 'visiting courses' are arranged wherever and whenever East Europeans invite them. These are the beginnings of a dialogue that, it is hoped, will illumine the values needed by democracies in both East and West.

POLAND: Prof Stanislaw Stomma, veteran Polish thinker and parliamentarian, talks at Caux with an Italian Member of the European Parliament

LITHUANIA (right to left): Prof Vytautas Landsbergis, first President of post-Communist Lithuania, with Douglas Johnston of the Center for Strategic and International Studies in Washington, and Jakob Kellenberger of the Swiss Department of Foreign Affairs

THE CZECH REPUBLIC: Dr Jaroslava Moserová, head of UNESCO in Prague, playwright and diplomat, gives a Caux Lecture on 'Those who left and those who stayed behind'

RUSSIA: academics and writers at a seminar on the 'moral lessons of Soviet history'

(left) Two veterans of the siege of Stalingrad meet at Caux, Moscow journalist Viktor Rodionov and Heinz Krieg of Berlin

(above right) Russian Human Rights Commissioner Sergei Kovalyov said, 'We Russians have no sense of our Russian guilt... Without looking into the past properly, I don't believe we can look into the future with clarity'

(right) Father Innekenty Pavlov of the Open Orthodox University, Moscow

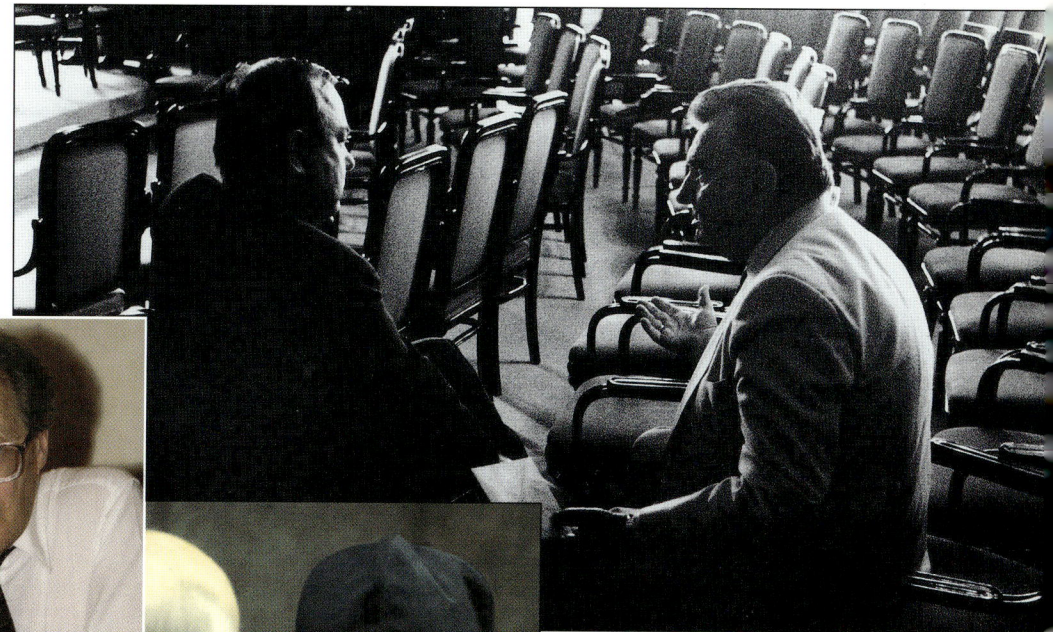

BOSNIA (above): Among those from former Yugoslavia, a citizen from Sarajevo and an emigré who decided to return discuss the situation

19

Forgiveness, a different dynamic

By the late 1940s the Caux community had realised that their job would extend far beyond Europe, and involve the healing of a deeper range of global divisions.

Japan, as well as Germany, needed to find a distinctive role in the post-war family of nations. Her war had ended like none other in history, with two atom bombs. An era had begun that would forever change the parameters of conflict.

On all sides, too, colonised peoples were pressing for an end to European control of huge areas of Asia and Africa. Millions had suffered racial and ethnic hurts.

So could justice be achieved? And could forgiveness generate a creative dynamic?

21

Opening 'a new page' in Japanese history...

Some commentators still believe that Japanese have made insufficient attempts to express regret for wartime atrocities. But in the 1950s, prominent Japanese who had visited Caux made considerable efforts to set relationships right with their former enemies.

In June 1950 some 70 Japanese were in Caux together. The most representative group to travel overseas since the war, it included the governors of seven provinces, six members of the Diet from the major parties, the Mayors of Hiroshima and Nagasaki, and industrial and labour leaders. Prime Minister Yoshida, farewelling them, recalled that in 1870 such a group of Japanese had travelled to the West and on

their return 'changed the course of Japanese life. I believe that when this delegation returns you too will open a new page in our history.'

In Washington on 24 July, on their way home from Caux, they were welcomed by Vice-President Alben Barkley into the Senate chamber. Chojiro Kuriyama, the Diet member representing the Prime Minister, expressed 'our sincere regret that Japan has broken an almost century-old friendship between our two countries.' He was quoted in a *New York Times* editorial which said, 'For a moment we could see out of the present darkness into the years when all men may become brothers.' *The Saturday Evening Post*, in another editorial, wrote, 'Perhaps even Americans

could think up a few past occasions of which it could be safely admitted, "We certainly fouled things up that time."'

Such an interchange demonstrates the power of apology to open previously closed relationships. Nobody demanded these expressions of regret; and the significance of such apologies became clear to them through the healing of divisions between some of their number – like Katsuji Nakajima, who was on the executive of the leftist All Japan Metal Workers' Union, and Eiji Suzuki, the Osaka chief of police.

Nakajima had been in Hiroshima when the bomb fell, had been close to death for months and was still suffering the effects. He had thought of Suzuki as public enemy number one and was horrified to discover him on the plane. At Caux, he wrestled for days with his feelings, and finally went to Suzuki's room to tell him that he felt such hatred was wrong. The next day Suzuki said publicly to him, 'I was bowled over by your gesture,' and apologised for his feelings against socialists and communists.

Five years after atom bombs flattened their cities, the Mayors of Hiroshima and Nagasaki (below) **were among the Japanese on the charter aircraft to Caux.**
Following his visit Hiroshima's Mayor wrote on the monument in the heart of his city:
'Let all the souls here rest in peace – for we shall never repeat the evil'

Two Japanese Prime Ministers, Nobusuke Kishi *(second from left)* with Mrs Kishi, and Takeo Fukuda *(right)* with Mrs Fukuda, and former Minister of Home Affairs Saburo Chiba *(left)* at Caux in 1961

Senator Kato *(right)* who urged Kishi to first put right the past
Niro Hoshijima *(below)* expressing regrets for the war to Koreans

This spontaneous demonstration of a social chasm being bridged would have many echoes in the years ahead, as members of this and other delegations saw the point of setting right what had been wrong. One young Diet member, Yasuhiro Nakasone, who 32 years later was to become Prime Minister, wrote an article for his home town newspaper in which he said that the delegation had come to the conclusion that, after all, class war and confrontation were not necessary in industry. 'The ice in Japanese hearts,' he wrote with a certain flourish, 'was melted by the international harmony that transcends race and class in this great current of world history moving through the continents of America and Europe.'

In 1955, British author Peter Howard drew on his experience of MRA in a musical play about a divided world, *The Vanishing Island*. It toured 18 countries on four continents within three months with a group of 244 people from 28 nations, arriving at Caux for the summer conferences. Japanese parliamentarian Niro Hoshijima, who was later to be Speaker of the Diet, travelled with the play from Japan to The Philippines. After the first performance, he stepped forward. When the audience heard the Japanese language, they began to murmur angrily and were only silenced by the translation. 'The Japanese,' said Mr Hoshijima, 'must pay war reparations. But reparations are not enough. First of all we must humbly apologise for the past. That is why my Prime Minister urged me to come with this delegation. Please forgive us.' The audience responded with thunderous applause.

Public apologies in nine countries

In April 1957 a leading Japanese paper, *Yomiuri*, reported frank exchanges between Koreans and Japanese at an MRA gathering in The Philippines. Mr Hoshijima and the Socialist Senator, Mrs Shidzue Kato, agreed that she would ask the Prime Minister, Mr Kishi, questions about the Japanese-Korean relationship when he appeared before the Foreign Affairs Committee of the Upper House, questions for which Mr Hoshijima had prepared him. This led to the Prime Minister officially disowning a statement by a Japanese official that had incensed Korea.

Later that year, Mrs Kato heard that Mr Kishi was about to go on a trade mission around Asia, and decided that she must tell him of her experience that the first essential in building for the future was to put right the past. He was so taken with what she said that he told his aides to rewrite his speeches. On 18 December, the *Washington Evening Star*, in an editorial, called Mr Kishi's trip 'one of the most unusual missions ever undertaken by a statesman of his rank... He has visited no fewer than nine nations that Japan occupied or threatened with conquest after the attack on Pearl Harbour... And in each of these lands he has publicly apologised for his country's actions during the war.'

In Australia, Mr Kishi's apology at a lunch in Parliament House for 250 MPs and other leading citizens had profound results. The *Sydney Morning Herald* editorialised, 'We cannot afford the luxury of living in the bitter past... Kishi handled a delicate mission with skilful tact. His ice-breaking tour... could hardly have been a pleasant experience. But no one could have gone further in making official amends for the sins of his country.'

'One of the most unusual missions ever undertaken by a statesman of his rank'

... and a new chapter for emerging nations in Africa

At Caux in 1953, exiled Tunisian nationalist Mohammed Masmoudi had a letter from his mother, ending, 'God bless you, my son. God curse the French.' Also at Caux was a former Moroccan Pasha, Si Bekkai, who had resigned his post because the French had exiled the Sultan of Morocco to Madagascar. Feeling in both countries – and in Algeria – was at fever pitch.

In the atmosphere of Caux, they were able to talk from the heart with people like Irène Laure. Masmoudi wrote to his mother that she should continue to pray for him but should stop cursing the French.

By the end of 1955 both Tunisia and Morocco had negotiated their independence. Si Bekkai became Morocco's first Prime Minister. Masmoudi, Tunisia's first Ambassador to France, spoke in Washington alongside the French Secretary for Air in the Mendès-France government, Diomède Catroux. He said, 'Without Moral Re-Armament, we would be involved today in Tunisia in a war to the death against France. Tunisia would now be a second Indo-China.'

The world has been astonished by the changed relationship between black and white in South Africa. In the difficult years beforehand, the Caux community had a preview, which kept them optimistic. It developed from a meeting in Lusaka in 1953 between Dr William Nkomo and George Daneel. Nkomo had been the first President of the African National Congress Youth League, whose first Secretary was Nelson Mandela. Daneel had been a Springbok rugby hero, and was a dominee of the Dutch Reformed Church.

Nkomo used to say that his aim had been to drive every white man into the sea, but after he and Daneel talked through all that divided them, he said: 'I saw white men change. I saw black men change. So I decided to change. I am no less a revolutionary because I believe in God. I am now fighting with greater passion for a hate-free, fear-free, greed-free Africa, peopled by free men and women.'

'The arrogance of white men like me'

Daneel 'suddenly realised that it was the arrogance of white men like me which caused the bitterness in men like Nkomo. I had to apologise and ask God to forgive me.' He spoke alongside Nkomo at a multiracial public meeting in Cape Town's City Hall. His attitude angered Presidents Verwoerd and Vorster, but Daneel was not fazed, taking a chance in 1972 to tell the Synod of the Dutch Reformed Church that it must break with separateness and superiority.

In 1974, Daneel with others organised the apparently impossible – a week-long international multiracial conference in Pretoria.

Philip Vundla, a militant union organiser of the African mine-workers and a member of the ANC national executive, used to say, 'What you achieve by violence, you will need greater violence to maintain. Those who say the answer is bloodshed have other people's blood in mind, not their own. By all means let us change the laws. They are unbearable. But in some countries laws have been changed and yet violence has grown because people's motives remained the same.'

Agnes Leakey Hofmeyr grew up in one of the best-known Kenya settler families. In 1954, her father was buried alive by a Mau Mau group in a shallow grave with dogs and goats, on the slopes of Mt Kenya. He was chosen as a sacrifice because he was known as a good man.

Agnes struggled with her feelings for weeks – vengeful hatred against blacks, doubts that God existed. In one moment of depression, she opened her heart to the Holy Spirit. 'Through all the turmoil,' she writes, 'the thought came perfectly clearly, "Have no bitterness or hatred but fight harder than ever to bring a change of heart to black and white alike".' As she wrestled with this daunting thought 'through stormy nights of tears, more and more my thoughts focussed on what we whites had done in Kenya and what the Mau Mau men had told us of the treatment by whites that had driven them into revolt... Perhaps a key to

> *'What you achieve by violence, you will need greater violence to maintain. Those who say the answer is bloodshed have other people's blood in mind, not their own.'*

the question "How can I forgive?" is to look at another question, "How much do I need forgiveness?" '

In the following months hundreds of former Mau Mau, hearing that she and other whites were determined to face where they needed to change, abandoned their oaths and took a cleansing ceremony. A number of these came to Caux and worked with Agnes and her South African husband Bremer Hofmeyr to demonstrate that forgiveness and change were possible, even in situations of terror.

One evening, years later, the Hofmeyrs were having dinner at Caux with one of these former Mau Mau leaders, Stanley Kinga. He turned to Agnes and said, 'There is something I have never told you. I was one of the committee in the Mau Mau that chose your father to be a sacrifice and planned his death.'

Agnes was dumbfounded, but they were able to talk through all that had happened. 'Thank God,' she finally said to him, 'that we have both learned the secret of forgiveness or we could never sit here.'

To most playwrights it would have seemed a crazy scenario. Some 30 Africans had been at Caux for a week in 1955. Their spectacular clothes had lit up the halls of Mountain House. And now Frank Buchman wanted them to write a play. Their continent, he said to them, was not meant to be torn between East and West but to give something to both. Why not from the stage?

None of them was a playwright, but they were willing to try. They met after lunch and were soon in a vigorous debate about what should go into it. Somebody suggested a time of silence, and when they pooled their thoughts, they found they had a story about an African country throwing off the imperialist yoke and having to deal with tribal and factional struggles for power. Three of them, from Nigeria, Ghana and South Africa, each wrote an act.

They called it *Freedom* and the first performance was within a week. It was in London a week later, then in Paris and Bonn. Such was the response that the cast abandoned plans to return home and toured Europe. With the help of Swedish cameraman Rickard Tegström, *Freedom* was filmed in Nigeria as a full-scale feature with a cast of thousands. The film has been translated into many languages. A million people saw it in Swahili, mostly in open air showings, in the months before free Kenya's first elections.

In Zimbabwe, the 1970s were a decade of growing guerrilla warfare aimed at overthrowing white minority rule. Zimbabweans of all races attended Caux conferences. Many saw there how they could work for changes in attitude needed to give the country the chance of a multiracial future. They organised meetings all over the country. They met guerrilla leaders in the bush. One of them, Rev Arthur Kanodereka, was assassinated in the midst of a bold peace initiative. But this did not stop them. In 1979 a Cabinet Minister and four MPs met at Caux with exiles from the opposing parties. Among the many who found fresh hope through their work was a public servant, Joram Kucherera.

Meanwhile, diplomatic initiatives persuaded all sides to agree to a ceasefire and elections. Former enemies went to the ballot box; but among the white-led army were people preparing a coup d'état against the guerrilla leader, Robert Mugabe, if he won the elections. At this tense moment, Kucherera went to Mugabe, and to the leader of the white minority, Ian Smith, and proposed a meeting. Both sides were wary. But on the eve of the announcement of the results, Kucherera took Smith alone in his old Morris Minor car past Mugabe's armed guards, and the two men spent several hours talking.

Next day, when Mugabe was proclaimed winner, Smith announced that he had met Mugabe and found him a 'reasonable man'. He said he intended to remain in Zimbabwe, and urged other whites to stay too. Mugabe went on radio and said that Zimbabweans must 'beat their swords into ploughshares... I urge you, whether you are black or white, to join me in a new phase. Forgive others and forget.'

(Left to right):
Kenyans Stanley Kinga and Agnes Hofmeyr

A poster for the German version of the film *Freedom*

Zimbabweans Arthur Kanodereka and Alec Smith, son of the last Prime Minister of Rhodesia, came together to Caux: colleagues in a 'Cabinet of Conscience'

Taking action in the search for reconciliation

An hour standing before a firing squad, and six months imprisonment, could not break Eritrean Abeba Tesfagiorgis. But what she chose to break was her hatred against the 'contemptible informer' whose confession had led to her arrest. Relating her story of survival at Caux in 1993, she told how she had confronted the man, by then also a prisoner. 'I made it brief: "You shamelessly testified against me on just hearsay... I hated your guts. Now I forgive you. If it were not for these horrendous times, neither you nor I, nor any of our cell-mates, would be in prison."'

Now back in liberated Eritrea as founder/director of the Centre for Human Rights and Development, Tesfagiorgis believes, 'When we forgive, doors open. Doors that we never thought would open. Reconciliation takes time, but in the end you win as an individual, as a family, as a nation.'

(Left to right):
Abeba Tesfagiorgis from Eritrea; Ahmed Egal from Somalia

Three Somalis from three divided clans came to Caux in 1992 when their country and their hopes were shattered. 'Our people are broken in pieces like a glass broken on the floor. I have been paralysed by despair,' said a history professor.

One of the three, Ahmed Egal, was living in exile, having argued with his guerrilla leader over tactics and been imprisoned as a result. 'Here I got a new weapon in the battle for my country – freedom from fear and bitterness,' he said on his second visit to Caux in 1993. Between the two visits he had returned to Somalia and sought out his former leader, asking his forgiveness for his bitter opposition. After hours talking together, Egal had won his leader's 'full confidence' in an approach to other clans. In Caux for a third year, and at meetings in between, Egal and his fellow Somalis began working on a plan of action for the 'reconciliation of our bleeding country'.

When Hindu militants demolished a Muslim mosque in Ayodhya in 1992, many Indian cities were engulfed in communal violence. Sushobha Barve was among the Bombay citizens who formed a peace committee, liaising with State leaders and the police, to quell the riots. Peace committees were set up in many neighbourhoods. A high-caste Hindu, Barve went into Dharavi, Asia's largest slum, staying for a week with a Muslim family rather than returning to the safety of her own home. She has worked there since to reduce the tensions, as well as working with Bombay's police chief to 'break through the wall of distrust' between police and those affected by riots. In 20 precincts police-citizen committees have been set up. 'These have helped ordinary people on the fringes to take responsibility and tackle what is wrong,' she said at Caux.

Barve's commitment to communal healing has grown over years, within India and on visits to Pakistan and Bangladesh. During violence after Indira Gandhi had been assassinated, she tried to protect two Sikhs being dragged from a train by an angry mob who beat them and set them on fire. Barve herself was beaten. 'This shook me to the core,' she said. It set her building links with prominent Sikhs around the country. 'India's soul will not be at peace unless as a nation and as a people we go through an experience of repentance. All have suffered and all have a part in the causes of suffering.

Without repentance and forgiveness, there is no peace, and without peace, poverty and related issues can never be resolved.'

Flying to Caux from New Zealand in 1971, Canon Wi Te Tau Huata flew over the World War II Italian battlefield of Monte Cassino. As Chaplain of the 28th New Zealand Maori Battalion, Huata had buried hundreds of his countrymen on the mountain. He was awarded the Military Cross but was left with 'a cancer of bitterness' against all Germans.

Only hours later in Caux, one of the first people he met was German. At a special church service at Caux, he explained that for years he had been ineffective as a minister because of his bitterness. But now he had 'handed over to God for removal' his hatred of Germans. Then he asked all Germans present to join him 'not to die for an old world but to live and battle for a new one'.

He had earlier cut off one of his sons who married a Catholic. His letter from Caux asking forgiveness of his son and daughter-in-law re-united the family.

Catholics and

'God has laid on my heart the task of conciliation of the military and the civilian population of my country.'

Protestants from Belfast then invited him to Northern Ireland to meet people from both sides at a time of sectarian violence. Some years later, Huata led a group of veterans of the Maori Battalion to Germany, invited by Rommel's Afrika Korps for their reunion held in Mainz. 'I could never have made that journey without that experience at Caux,' he said.

A death squad was waiting for Guatemalan Eliézer Cifuentes as he drove into his home street one night. Deeply involved in the cooperative movement, he had become a target of powerful land-owning interests. Four car-loads of men fired on him as he fled. Wounded in one arm, he took shelter in the Costa Rican Embassy.

In exile, frustrated and bitter, he attended a seminar run by people from Caux and was challenged by the story of French socialist Irène Laure and her work for reconciliation. 'I saw the tigers of hatred in my own heart for the military whom I blamed for the attempt on my life, and for the US which I felt was backing them,' he said later. 'I had not practised the love that I had repeatedly preached. I found a renew-al inside that changed my desire for vengeance. Giving up hatred was a wonderful personal experience, but my danger was to leave it at that.'

Peace: not around the corner but bound to come

Courageously he has begun a dialogue with Guatemalan army officers, starting with those he blamed for ordering the attack against him, and with indigenous Mayan and white political leaders. 'God has laid on my heart the task of conciliation of the military and the civilian population of my country. Peace is not around the corner, but it is bound to come.'

The seminar which Cifuentes attended can be traced back to 1948, when a Costa Rican called Luis Alberto Monge met one of Caux's founders at an International Labour Organisation conference. In 1950 he went to Caux with three friends. In time each of them was elected President of Costa Rica. Supporting the Caux 50th anniversary in 1996, Monge wrote: 'The creation of a new conscience has become imperative for humanity... Nothing can be achieved in the road towards peace, liberty, justice and solidarity if there is no inner transformation in each human being.'

Programs in other Central American countries have included a 12-year interchange between Salvadoran and US jurists focussed on judicial ethics.

**(Left to right):
Sushobha Barve from India, Wi Te Tau Huata from New Zealand, and Eliézer Cifuentes, Guatemala**

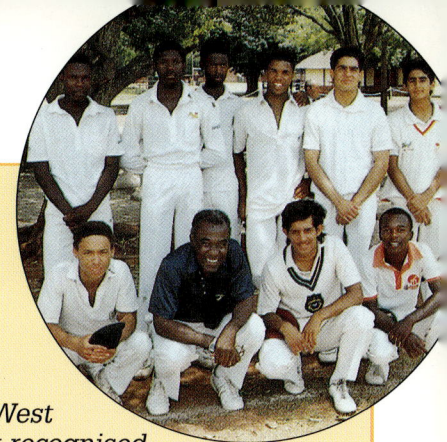

Conrad Hunte was Vice-Captain of the West Indies cricket team when the world first recognised their brilliance. He and his wife Patricia, formerly anchor-person for the evening TV news on a major channel in Atlanta, Georgia, moved to South Africa in 1991 so that Hunte could develop the skills of young black cricketers there. He said at Caux in 1994:

I am a black man. I come from a people who carry with us the memory of slavery. I was born in a tiny village on the island of Barbados in the West Indies where my father worked on a sugar plantation. The eldest of nine children, I know what it is to be poor. Cricket, for which I had a natural talent, was my way out. I ate, lived, dreamed and practised cricket to become one of the best in my country, and I rose from poverty to plenty, from obscurity to name and fame.

The doors to the future we all long for are barred and blocked by the unhealed wounds from the past. We have been flooded by seven rivers of hate – the industrial revolution and the problems in its wake, the traffic in slaves which deepened the gulf between the races, the legacy of colonialism and imperialism, the West's humiliation of China, the breakdown of family life and the alienation of many young people, the deep divisions between people of faith, and the ideological rejection of God.

If we are to go forward as human beings, we will need forgiveness by those who have suffered and repentance by those who have caused the suffering. When forgiveness meets repentance, a new energy, a dynamic, creative synergy is released that the world has scarcely begun to tap.

The unhealed memory of past wounds causes us to be more conscious of how and where others have hurt us and are hurting us. This lack of healing blinds us to how and where we have hurt and are still hurting others.

We can be an instrument of peace and nation-building when, as individuals and representatives of our ethnic groups and nations, we acknowledge our hurt or our guilt, accept forgiveness or give it, and create this new synergy together.

Conrad Hunte

Encounters of a global kind

A Russian journalist, who first came to Caux in 1969 as a convinced Communist, returned years later in 1993. In one meeting he found himself sitting next to a Czech – on the 25th anniversary of the Warsaw Pact's brutal ending of the Prague Spring. He only realised this when, at one point, everyone was asked to turn to his neighbour and relate one experience of healing or bridge-building. The bridge-building began at that moment.

A Northern Irish Catholic, for five years interned without trial, was introduced to a Fijian Ratu (chief) who was scheduled to speak with him on the same platform about forgiveness. The Ratu's jaw dropped. 'What day were you interned? What neighbourhood?' The Ratu, like many of his countrymen, had served in the British Army, as a sergeant-major. At the very moment the Irishman had been arrested, the Ratu was on duty in a nearby barracks. Their animated conversation spilled over onto the platform for all to hear.

You never know who you might meet in Caux...

The world takes on a different aspect...

*I*ndeed on any one day at Caux you might find yourself eating a meal with a New York media executive, a fashion designer from Lagos, a student from Hanoi, a Brazilian ecologist, a British car-worker or a Swedish classical guitarist.

In the interaction – of experiences, attitudes and values – there is often challenge. Perhaps not as dramatic as for the Russian and Czech, or the Fijian and the Northern Irish Catholic. And, for most of us, less anguishing than those challenges faced by Abeba Tesfagiorgis, Agnes Hofmeyr or Wi Te Tau Huata. But whether we like it or not, in today's world of struggle and differences, we are all faced with choices. Any step towards people from whom we may have kept our distance, any opening of our hearts and minds towards a reality denied or previously unseen, becomes a step towards a more global community. The world takes on a different aspect. And we find new ways of taking action.

Significant for sanity

Back in 1953 an ambitious young Australian Member of Parliament, Kim Beazley, came for what he thought would be one week in Caux, but stayed for seven. 'I had to admit that what I saw at Caux was far more significant for the peace and sanity of the world than anything being done at that time in Australian politics.' Beazley soon grasped that the process at Caux was not just 'cheap subscribing to principles' but a 'decisive act, a turning of the will'. He began by 'turning the searchlight of absolute honesty on to my motives', and he made it practical in a way which one correspondent back home wrote was 'political dynamite'. One reality impinged on Beazley's thinking during that visit to Caux: that if he lived a purity of motive, he would be used in the rehabilitation of the Australian Aboriginal race. For over 30 years in politics he was at the forefront of land rights legislation and far-reaching educational reforms for Aboriginals.

'There is sanity from the Holy Spirit beyond human ideas of justice,' said Beazley. 'This is the essence of intelligent statesmanship.'

'Not just cheap subscribing to principles but a decisive act, a turning of the will'

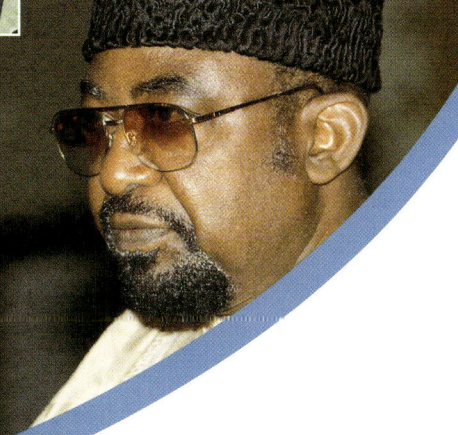

Clockwise from top left:

Women from Fiji and the Sudan become friends;

Young people from Sierra Leone, Britain and Malaysia discover each other's worlds;

Chief David Crowchild from western Canada;

The Emir of Kano from northern Nigeria;

Jacky Minard, politician and community activist from Roubaix in France, talks about unemployment;

Spanning continents, a conversation between people from Cameroon, Spain and Laos;

(Centre photo) **Niketu Iralu of the Naga people from India's North-East with Cambodia's Buddhist patriarch Venerable Maha Ghosananda**

Scrubbed, chopped, spiced and served...

'I saw nobody giving orders,' a 13-year-old teenager remarked after a week at Caux. 'There was no boss. Everyone seemed to feel responsible for others. This was new for me.'

For a week a Russian professor of philosophy volunteered to cook on a shift – and learnt as much about responsibility and reconciliation as he had in the conference forums. 'All Russian philosophers should come to this place,' he said with a grin, 'and all should work in the kitchen!' A Nigerian woman joked that she comes to Caux because it is the only place she finds African men in the kitchen.

Whether preparing meals or cleaning rooms, conference participants join in the work, assisting a small professional staff. Even the night-watchmen and accountants are volunteers. While each person contributes towards a standard accommodation fee – some more, some less – all contribute towards the teamwork that makes the operation of this large conference centre possible.

Many who come to Caux carry away with them this sense of responsibility for its practical aspects. Danes and Norwegians have provided food and catering material. In gratitude for what so many Swedes had found at Caux three Swedish couples about to get married decided to ask not for wedding presents but for contributions to the redesigning of the whole dining room – ceiling, lighting, windows and a covering carpet. The chairs and tables of Swedish birch are still sturdy and attractive after nearly 40 years of use. In the Seventies, a group of youth volunteered a winter to help improve the room's acoustics. The Finnish fresco painter Lennart Segerstråle and the Swedish artist Joel Mila gave a mural and major paintings for the dining room (see page 35) and many other pieces of Nordic art adorn the corridors.

Even the night-watchmen and accountants are volunteers

Clockwise from bottom left:

A team of cooks, representing many countries and cuisines, prepares a meal for 500;

Washing the dishes is where the action really takes place;

Preparing vegetables is taken on by workers in their 'third age';

Flowers, grown on the property, are a delight throughout Mountain House;

A Scottish electronics buff operates the sound controls;

Children and their minders learn together;

(centre photo) Handling up to eight languages between them, translators simultaneously interpret meetings, films and plays

With artistic sensibility and dramatic implications

One of the first things that caught the eye of the Swiss who looked gingerly at the old Palace Hotel in 1946 was the ballroom. 'It would make a wonderful theatre,' thought Robert Hahnloser, and work on converting it began as soon as the contract was signed. For 'life's a stage', and the Caux theatre has conveyed plenty of its drama.

In the past 50 years it has seen hundreds of productions, from one-man shows to musicals with casts of dozens, from highly-polished professional presentations to the more home-grown. As well as European comedy and drama in many languages, plays have also been written by Asians, Africans, North and South Americans.

At the end of a week's meeting of young people, a Hungarian violinist mounted the platform and in halting English said: 'Instead of words, I want to play for you my violin.' She performed *Meditation on Thaïs* with such feeling that her young audience – more accustomed to Madonna than Massenet – burst into applause. A few evenings later the same audience was on their feet resonating with a Black American soul group.

Some productions have gone from Caux onto stages around the world. Actors and artists have also met in forums, interpreting the social and spiritual implications of their work. In recent years such forums have been held in Poland, Lithuania and Russia as well.

From South Africa, Britain and America, a jazz trio improvises in the *Caux-Café*

Satirising Cold War prejudices, British playwright Peter Howard's *Through the Garden Wall* was performed by this professional Italian cast in Caux after touring Italy. Swiss theatre director Egon Karter commented: 'Howard has left behind the psychological drama of Ibsen and Sartre... It is a shock therapy for the human reason and the human heart.'

French actor Michel Orphelin returned to Caux each year for 12 years with *Poor Man Rich Man*, a one-man musical by Hugh Steadman Williams on the life of St Francis of Assisi

Four dancers from four cultures, four religions, introduce the theme of *Song of Asia* which toured Europe from Caux, with a cast of young people from 14 Asian nations

Along one wall of Caux's dining room is a vast mural by Finnish painter Lennart Segerstråle *(above)*, one of the Nordic artists who have contributed works to Caux. 'Art of the future must be dangerous to evil,' said Segerstråle.

Soon after the Iron Curtain crumbled, artists from eastern and central Europe performed in Caux, including members of The Moscow Arts Theatre *(above)* and Russian pianist Victor Rjabchikov *(right)*

Stalling between Two Fools, a satirical cabaret written and acted by Philip and Vendela Tyndale-Biscoe *(left)*

'The global and the intimate linked in a surprising way'

French philosopher Gabriel Marcel, in his book *Fresh Hope for the World*, observed the meetings between many people at Caux and called them 'decisive encounters... or to put it more precisely, the act by which one person's consciousness can open up in the presence of another person's consciousness'. Marcel's book describes many of these encounters as fundamentally bringing an experience of change: 'not just subjective change, but a radical change of the personality'.

'Most striking of all, you find here the global and the intimate linked in a surprising way.'

Writing in *Le Figaro*, Marcel said of Caux: 'I know of no other place where you come into such clear touch with the only freedom which is worthwhile, the freedom of the children of God... It is a seed. Those in whom the seed has been sown are changed from within. That is to say that they have seen evidence of the light of the absolute and, moved by this evidence, they become capable of overthrowing the barriers which separate them from themselves and from each other. It is a hope... for without this spirit which brings men together in a complete moral transparency, there is surely no alternative to the vicious circles of deception and mutual revenge.'

Members of Parliament don't have much time to think. So I come to Caux to think, to contemplate in this extraordinary place on the mountain which inspires you to reflect about yourself and your relationship with others.... I experience here a kind of face to face with the whole world, with myself, with God. Here you will find a great will to listen. We learn to respect the other, because we learn to listen; we learn to understand, because we listen.
Jean-Marie Daillet, French diplomat and politician

We all want the happiness which comes from peace of mind. Peace of mind is destroyed by anger and hatred, so we first must struggle with them. They are our real enemies.... Tolerance and forgiveness are the key methods for minimising hatred. You cannot feel hatred or disrespect towards your guru, so you cannot learn tolerance and forgiveness from him. You can only learn these things from your enemy. When you meet him, that is the golden opportunity to test how much you practise what you believe.
The Dalai Lama, on his visit to Caux in 1983

It was very hard for me to forgive the Khmer Rouge for what they did to my beloved country. Millions were killed. I lost my husband and all my relatives except my children. You can say 'I forgive' but you do not know if you have until the problem is there in front of you. In 1988 I went with other educators to a Khmer Rouge camp in Thailand. My heart was not hard; my voice was the same. I knew then that my wounds were healed, that my forgiveness was real. The burden of revenge which I carried for a decade was lightened. Without meditation I would not be strong enough to avoid falling into the three fires of greed, anger and foolishness.
**Cambodian educator Renée Pan,
who returned to Cambodia under the UN**

Abuse in the reservation where I grew up, and the self-hate it causes, are symptoms of the pain that my people have been through. I got tired of hating myself, of 'being a victim'. That was the beginning of healing... I was able to see my pain as a gift. The Creator has given my people strong spiritual-cultural traditions to deal with these pains. There is nothing wrong with asking for help. It is a sign of strength rather than of weakness. We must speak the truth to find healing. I cannot change the world into which I was born, but I can change my life now.
**Gaaxstalas of the N'amgis Territory of the Kwakwaka'wak
Nation, Canada, speaking of her childhood in a
dysfunctional alcoholic family**

In Norway we've tried to build a society where everything is looked after – but pain and suffering find their way into our life anyway. Instead of facing the pain we use a lot of strength trying to avoid and deny it. Pain walked into my own life with my husband's illness. We felt like our plans and dreams were crushed. I learnt that when I accept that pain is a natural part of life, it is not as frightening anymore. In meeting pain, you also meet your own limits. And in meeting my limits, I have to turn to God. Facing my own and others' suffering is one of the most essential sources of growth – something in our country we might have to learn again.

Camilla Nelson, Norwegian artist

'Modern man lacks silence. He doesn't lead his life, he is led by events. It is a race against the clock. Even God Himself can't get anything else in. So it is vital to make space somewhere... Silence has a power which forces you to go deeper into yourself.'

Paul Tournier, Swiss physician and author

I understand the rejection and hopelessness that many of my West Indian people feel. But when we start burning cars and throwing petrol bombs, I realise how much we have lost our sense of values... What does one do to change things? The desire for quick money, to make a million, was the aim of my life. My aim now is to create a society of justice and equal opportunity, where the challenge of absolute honesty, purity, unselfishness and love is accepted by black and white alike.... If you're not mixing, you're not healing.

Miguel Richards, Chairman of *Bridge Builders*, a community-relations network in a southern suburb of London, UK

I have long ago taken to heart to be a bridge between East and West, Islam and other faiths. In 1991, as I looked at all the resentments caused by the Gulf War, I realised it was no longer a question of expressing my anger and hurt at the world's negative reaction to Arabs, but was I prepared to live differently enough to bring about reconciliation and healing? There's a price that we each have to pay. For me as a Muslim, it means living my faith with a depth and a quality that will change the West's false impressions of Islam. The actual word 'Muslim' means to submit your will to God. So it becomes the basis for everything that you do, every day... If we stopped talking about the theory and actually lived our faiths, we would be surprised by our ability to learn from one another and how our lives are enriched by diversity.

Omnia Marzouk, Egyptian paediatrician in Liverpool, UK

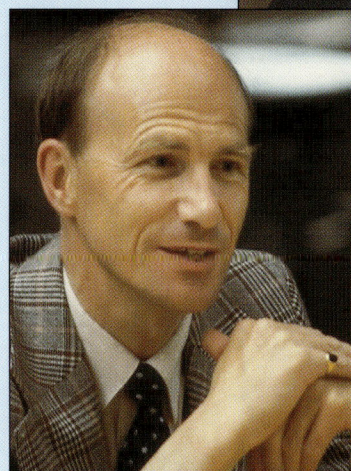

The legitimate desire to eradicate pain and suffering, the bending of our minds to crack the secrets of life, can be used, if faith and its morality are absent, to turn the world towards the illusory goal of a material heaven on earth. We must face the fact that our sophisticated materialistic progress, which we regard as the best of our societies, could destroy our souls. The effect of a material world is to make us want to measure faith and religion in terms of human success. But the Christian life of faith is about a relationship. It is about love not duty. All the tasks are secondary, even if necessary. All else flows from the desire to make that primary loyalty, primary love, primary relationship the demonstrable, observable, transparent goal of our lives.

John Lester, British doctor and author

Out on a limb, but looking for solutions

Caux's programs in the Nineties are potentially as relevant to today's world as those in the Forties. As well as general assemblies in which any searcher can participate, there has been much careful specialisation in an attempt to bring the possibilities of change in people's attitudes and motives into today's crucial economic and social debates.

This has made Caux the creative centre of many informal alliances between people who want to find what to do about the needs that confront them and their communities. 'Joint responsibility in action' was how a South African described it. He had looked for a chief administrator and subordinates, but found none.

Some of these initiatives are outlined in the following pages. Many more are unknown — a tapestry of experiences and action woven by people who followed some thread of conviction they found at Caux and were willing to go out on a limb to make it happen.

Tackling the crisis in cities, home to half of humanity

*I*n 1900, 14 per cent of the world's population lived in cities. By 2000 half the world will. Some cities are larger than entire nations, and are home to people from a multitude of nationalities, races and creeds. In the developing countries, millions have no home but the pavement, no water supply, no sewerage, no education. Indeed everywhere cities are facing crises. Global urbanisation has become a 'social time-bomb', said Dr Raymond Bakke, founder of International Urban Associates based in Chicago.

Bakke was key-note speaker in 1990 at the first of the 'cities consultations' which have taken place at Caux and in 30 cities on four continents. These have been initiated by people like Bernard Gauthier, a police chief and later deputy chief of France's Commission on the Integration of Immigrants. Political or administrative actions alone would never change things, said Gauthier. To get to grips with 'the visible causes of our crisis – poverty, family break-up, crime, drugs, racism – but also tackle the underlying structural ills' will take new motives: in short, a change in people.

'People are not leopards'

Evidence of such basic change is brought by people like a teacher who helped create 'a network for the exchange of knowledge' linking 20,000 immigrants and marginalised people in France; and like the founder of the Bridge Park Business and Leisure Centre, training teenage dropouts for employment from an old bus depot in Brent, London. 'We look at criminals and say "a leopard can't change his spots", but people are not leopards,' argued Leonard Johnson, who himself underwent a spiritual change in prison. 'We can't afford the stereotype perceptions which write people off.'

Citizens from Pasadena, a city within Los Angeles, described Day One, a highly-effective community-based coalition for drug prevention and rehabilitation, and Young and Healthy, which ensures health-care for children in need. Both programs are run by an Office for Creative Connections working on the principle of 'listening and revealing the city to itself so that the community takes care of itself'.

The initiators of Black Teens for Advancement, a 4,000-strong student initiative in Atlanta, USA, are interviewed by journalist Patricia Hunte. In its first year BTA was credited with a 40 per cent decrease in violent crime in Atlanta's public high schools

Walking through the hidden history of Richmond, Virginia: 'Here is where the end of racism should begin.'

*W*ithin months of the 1992 Los Angeles 'uprising' which shook the USA, 70 Americans at Caux realised that a different response was needed to 'the toxic issue of race which seeps through our national agenda'.

Mayor Walter T Kenney and a delegation from Richmond, Virginia, undertook to host an 'honest conversation on race, reconciliation and responsibility' in their city, capital of the Confederacy of southern states during the Civil War. Less than a year later over 1,000 people from 56 cities and 20 countries met in Richmond for a conference on *Healing the heart of America*. The highlight was an unprecedented two-mile walk through the city's hidden history – to such sites as Manchester Docks where for a century thousands of slaves had been unloaded in chains. 'Here, where racism in its worst form started in this country, is where the end should begin,' said an organiser.

The 'honest conversation' has sparked Hope in the Cities, an inter-racial, multi-faith coalition growing in a dozen American cities. Building on models of hope and effective cross-city partnerships, they aim to establish 'not new programs but a new process'. They suggest four ways to do this:

Human development in Rio's shanty-towns

Chicago's Ray Bakke with Hari Shukla, director of the Race Equality Council in Newcastle upon Tyne, UK, where a multi-language phone bank, police-community councils and inter-faith cooperation are evidence of Shukla's vision for his city

- Within the group which is attempting to bring healing, model the change and relationships that it is asking of the wider community;
- Be inclusive. Do not demonize opponents. Risk approaching as potential allies those who are difficult to work with;
- Hold up a vision of what community can be. Difficulties, if faced, can become assets;
- Recognise that the energy and will for constructive change, including political will, can only come through a transformation in the human spirit, starting with each one of us.

Working among France's immigrants, Fr Christian Delorme describes the dialogue between different faiths which in today's multi-ethnic societies has become essential

Brazil's Luiz Pereira (*below left*) and Euclides da Silva (*bottom*)

*L*ack of adequate housing is an enormous social need in many cities, particularly in the developing world. In Rio de Janeiro, for instance, 300,000 people arrive every year, mostly from rural villages, and go to live in one of 600 shanty towns, or *favelas*. Housing anything up to three million people, they are centres of gang violence and the drug trade.

But the work of grassroots community associations in these *favelas* is one of the great human development stories of our time, dating back 40 years.

In 1955 Nelson Marcellino de Carvalho and Damasio Cardoso were leaders of two rival unions in the port of Rio de Janeiro. One morning during a 54-day strike, Cardoso went to Marcellino's warehouse armed with two revolvers and a knife, intending to kill him if he didn't give way. Marcellino turned the tables by admitting where he had been wrong and suggesting they join forces. A more honest relationship began to emerge, enabling the creation of one new union.

They visited Caux together. The pattern of strikes and corruption came to an end and the port's performance improved. Their story, documented in a film, *Men of Brazil*, was shown widely through the *favelas*.

One of those who saw it was a *favela* community president, Euclides da Silva. The dockers struck him as being 'effective and fearless'. After many conversations with them da Silva decided to 'take an honest look at my own life'. He was secretly profiteering from his constituents by buying electricity at four cruzeiros a kilowatt hour and selling it to them at 11. He and his rival, who also held an electricity concession, had made several attempts to kill each other. Over time they became friends. He called a meeting of the *favela* where he admitted his profiteering and resigned. To his surprise he was re-elected, and the new spirit of trust that resulted made possible a united proposal by *favela* presidents to the state government for a major housing scheme.

Another *favela* leader, Luiz Pereira, experiencing the same personal change as Euclides, won the confidence of the State Minister of Interior of Rio, who authorised a project to build blocks of flats, rehousing thousands of *favela* inhabitants. In the 22 years since they moved out of their shack, Pereira and his wife Edir have helped countless leaders of the community associations find unity and stand firm against corruption. Many of them have begun projects to rebuild houses and to care for children in their communities. Their work has inspired two taxi cooperatives committed to honest dealings with their passengers. The Pereiras meet regularly with those in the *favelas* and have brought many of the leaders to Caux.

Reaching for the society of tomorrow...

'This is the first time anyone asked us what we thought,' said a Romanian student. 'And they took our ideas seriously.' She was one of a team of young people organising a conference on 'bringing down walls' of prejudice between races and nationalities.

'Many young people ask, what is the point of knowing all that goes on in the world?' said a Swiss student teacher. 'The news so easily drowns us; and it always seems to be bad news. But here in Caux, I see the point of knowing: so as to do something.'

The input of her generation brings creativity and energy to many areas of Caux's life. An 'inter-generational dialogue' one year had young children and octogenarians 'talking about the deepest things in our lives with total strangers', in the words of one somewhat surprised 50-year-old. Another year there was 'a journey of exploration together... connecting the intimate and global' dimensions of living.

A British law student, at Caux, thought his generation needed to look deeper at the society of tomorrow. Back in London, he talked to two friends. Soon he was joined by an artist, a research scientist, a cartoonist, a tour-guide from Paris, an American stage director living in Sweden... and others. 'We differ in race, religion, socio-economic background and political viewpoint,' they said. But within 12 months they had planned an innovative session at Caux to 'tackle some hot issues' their generation faces.

No longer a sleep-walker

Their process focused on questions of identity, conflict and the need for transformation. After 'case studies' each morning by such people as a Bosnian sociology professor and a Buddhist monk, individuals and groups could be seen scattered around Caux, wrestling with tough questions. Confronted by a powerful one-man play about race called *The Invisible Man*, a young white South African – fed up with implied accusations of being a racist – told people from 37 countries, 'I am deeply sorry for what people have done to those of different race or culture... I am no longer a sleep-walker in my world.'

Role playing mediation in a Third World country, Caux Scholars focus on the transformation of conflict

'This course has changed my notion of what it means to understand another person,' said a Harvard University undergraduate.

The Caux Scholars Program, which runs concurrently with the Caux summer conferences, examines the sociological, psychological, spiritual and ethical dimensions of peace-making and peace-building. Developed over several years by academics and practitioners in the field of conflict resolution and mediation, the course consists of case studies, simulations, interactive learning and lectures. Faculty and guest lecturers are drawn from around the world and include people with extensive experience in teaching, public affairs and conflict resolution.

Assessing the '95 course, Malaysian editor and environmental activist N Nithiyananthan wrote that it 'combined academic work with an environment that was highly intellectual and spiritual, facilitated physical activity, and enabled social interaction'.

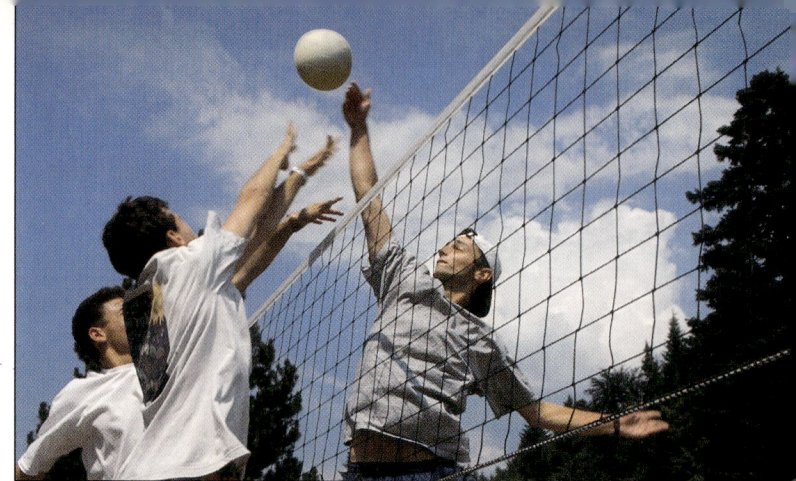

British law student Kumar Raval (above) and friends wrestle with questions of identity and conflict, whilst looking towards 'the society of tomorrow'

... in industry, business and human relationships

Among the forums in session is one for young business leaders

Lina and Maurice Mercier (*above*), and Robert Carmichael (*right*)

Francis Blanchard, for 16 years Director General of the ILO, said that Caux has 'an atmosphere where problems can be approached in complete frankness'. From its very first days thousands from shop floor and boardroom have sought fresh perspectives there. The phrase 'it's not who's right but what's right' has become a maxim of Caux – a simple idea that encourages people to search for objectivity and cast aside prejudices. Here are two examples:

Taizo Ishizaka, President of the electronic giant, Toshiba, was at Caux in 1950, and the company still sends delegations. In 1953, its industrial relations chief, Ryozaburo Kawahara, and the union head, Etsuro Yamamura, faced a tense situation with a threatened strike when they returned from Caux. The two men were opposites: Kawahara a quiet, dapper man, and Yamamura, brawny and flamboyant, with an enormous waxed moustache. But they talked through their hostile attitudes and became friends. The company and union had no formal contract and negotiated twice a year. But as they joined the negotiations, each side stopped wrangling and listened to the other. Agreement was reached the day before the deadline. One plant, running eight million yen in the red each month, was about to be closed but within a few weeks had begun to run three million yen in the black.

A new national credo

Similar results could be seen in other big electrical companies, heavy industry and the national railways, just as the era of Japanese creativity and confidence was dawning. A new national credo was being woven, from many different strands, that fitted the needs of an intensely homogeneous society looking for an aim that would take all its energy. Those who had been at Caux contributed by organising hundreds of meetings to discuss their new concepts, and writing and performing plays to dramatise them.

To the union president at the Ishikawajima shipyards, Renzo Yanagisawa, for instance, Caux felt 'like the conscience of the world, the place where body and soul are cleansed'. He persuaded his executive to put their cards on the table with management by stating openly what they wanted in wages and fringe benefits, and giving their analysis of the company's position. The company president, Toshiwo Doko, did likewise. Yanagisawa went on to head the national union and was later elected a Senator. Doko became Chairman of the Keidanren (Japan's National Federation of Economic Organisations).

Maurice Mercier and Robert Carmichael were trade union leader and employer respectively in the French textile industry. Mercier had been a Communist from the Depression until the end of World War II. They had been on the opposite sides of the barricades during the Popular Front strikes of 1936 and met again at Caux in 1950. Mercier was amazed to see how Carmichael's perspectives had altered. In 1951 and 1953, after 80 factory delegations of management and workers had attended MRA conferences at Mercier's initiative, French textile managers and workers signed two landmark agreements. The second of these was so anti-inflationary that it was described by Prime Minister Pinay as 'one of the first solid achievements on the road of the change which is indispensable to the economic survival of the country'.

Carmichael made use of this experience to pioneer a new approach to the use of raw materials. As head of the European jute industry, he secured a much fairer price for the producers of jute in the Indian subcontinent. This was the first free negotiation about the price of a raw material, and a milestone in the relations between the First and Third Worlds.

43

Beyond trade war to global responsibilities

A dialogue involving, say, British miners, Wall Street bankers, Black South African union leaders, Rio de Janeiro dockers, Indian production-line workers and Swedish delegations from Volvo and Electrolux, is bound to produce many insights. From 1974 the long tradition of such meetings became formalised in annual Conferences for Business and Industry in Caux. Delegations have come from many former Communist states, and seminars have been organised as a result in such places as Poland, Estonia and Siberia.

They have covered a wide range of themes – the environment, poverty and development, industrial and international relations, unemployment, and information technology.

In 1986 there were signs that Japan, Europe and the United States might be on the verge of a catastrophic trade war. This distressed Dr Frederik Philips, one-time President of the global giant Philips Electronics, and Olivier Giscard d'Estaing, Vice-Chairman of the French graduate management school, INSEAD. They decided to gather the best people they knew in the three areas to get down to brass tacks about what could be done. They called the gathering the Caux Round Table.

Wary of Japan-bashing

The Japanese were wary of the 'Japan-bashing' they had felt in the world media. Even in the first sessions some Westerners got heated. Toshihiko Yamashita, former President of Matsushita Electric (National Panasonic), said at the end that they had thought they were coming to a heavenly place, 'but then felt we were being pushed into hell'. Fortunately the idea came up that the best kind of honesty was about oneself – and heaven was rediscovered. With the result that the relationship between those present lost any terrors it might have had because the dangerous territory had been crossed.

The experiment was judged so valuable that the Round Table has met twice yearly ever since, in Caux every summer for three days, and between these sessions at a range of locations from Tokyo to Washington DC to Guandong Province in China.

In July 1994, the Caux Round Table published a set of Principles for Business. London's *Financial Times* commented that 'it contains nothing which will surprise enlightened companies. However, it is thought to be the first time a document of this kind has attracted influential supporters from Europe, Japan and the US.'

A global standard for business

The unique thing about the Principles is that they attempt to provide a global standard for business. They consciously embody ideals from Europe – the concept of respect for human dignity; from Japan – *kyosei*, best translated as living and working together for the common good; and from the US – the Minnesota Principles for Corporate Behavior, which recognise that all the 'stakeholders' in a corporation need to be respected. These stakeholders include customers, employees, stockholders, suppliers and local communities.

The Caux Round Table's Principles cover the interests of these various stakeholders with 38 different points. There are seven general Principles, including Support for Multilateral Trade, Respect for the Environment and Avoidance of Illicit Operations.

A sample:

'Principle 3: Business Behaviour: Beyond the Letter of Law Toward a Spirit of Trust.
While accepting the legitimacy of trade secrets, businesses should recognise that sincerity, candor, truthfulness, the keeping of promises and transparency contribute not only to their own credibility and stability but also to the smoothness and efficiency of business transactions, particularly on the international level.'

Tashihiko Yamashita of Matsushita Electric

Ryuzaburo Kaku of Canon with Dr Frederik Philips of Philips Electronics at the Caux Round Table

The Caux Round Table in session: 'committed to energising business and industry as a vital force for innovative global change'

Olivier Giscard d'Estaing, a Caux Round Table convenor, listens to Martin Bangemann, Vice-President of the EC, at a meeting in Brussels

David Rockefeller *(second right)* with Frank Stankard of Chase Manhattan, USA, and Isamu Sakamoto of Sumitomo Electric *(left)*, and Fujio Mitarai, now President of Canon, Japan *(second from left)*

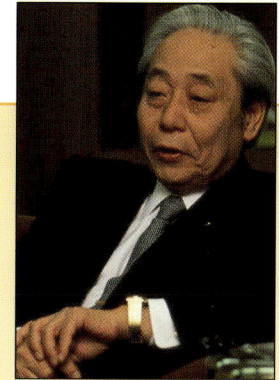

The Caux Round Table in China welcomed by Zhu Senlin, Governor of Guangdong Province, the centre of high economic growth; and *(below)* in a Harijan colony where Mahatma Gandhi often stayed in New Delhi

Ryuzaburo Kaku,
Chairman of Canon, Japan

Addressing global imbalances

Japan must change, and with all urgency. Japan's national system has reached its limits, and a new national concept of kyosei, living and working together for the common good, is needed. Japan must build an open system that contributes to the whole world.

In my view corporations evolve through four stages:
1. Purely capitalistic companies stimulate economies. However the management and owners share the benefits and care very little for employees. This situation gives rise to labour disputes.
2. Companies where management and workers are united in working for the prosperity of the corporation and both have a share in the profits. These companies can solve labour disputes but can draw criticism from local companies and do little to solve problems in the local community.
3. Companies assuming local social responsibilities which respect their own stakeholders and the local community. However such organisations can cause international friction because they care only for the national interests of the country in which they operate. They care little about global problems.
4. Companies assuming global social responsibilities care for their direct stakeholders, the local community and the world in which they operate.

There are all sorts of imbalances on this Earth, between the rich and poor, in international trade and between advanced and developing nations. The largest imbalance, however, is the problem of the environment, which can also be seen as an imbalance between generations. A corporation should endeavour to eliminate these imbalances. It has a network all round the world, and must therefore act as a leading player in such innovation.

Ryuzaburo Kaku

In situations of entrenched conflict, creating an interplay of experience...

An Irish politician, after lengthy discussions on his country's sectarian conflict, told a British friend that, if he came to Caux, he would rather interact with people from other crisis areas, such as the Lebanon or South Africa, than to meet more Irish.

Since 1991 Lebanese, South Africans, Irish – and many others from the world's trouble spots – have met at conferences in Caux. A dynamic process has evolved, encapsulated in its theme: *Regions in crisis, regions in recovery – learning from one another.*

As Dr Yusuf Omar Al-Azhari, a former Somali ambassador to the USA, said: 'It is important not to be left alone with your problems... Places like this are a bridge for new ideas. Just bringing 57 nationalities together, with their different cultures and politics, is a very valuable function.'

'The extra factor here at Caux is honesty and transparency,' added his countryman Osman Jama Ali, a former minister. 'When you are able to admit where you were wrong, the tension goes.' In this way Somalis of different clans have pursued an agenda of reconciliation with others from the Horn of Africa.

Pledged to refuse bribes

An African educator was helped by a Cambodian on how to 'win over' opponents. A Grand Chief of Canada's Mohawk people found South Africa's experience gave him ideas of processes for handling Canada's internal conflicts. A 'Clean Election' movement in Taiwan, supported by 670,000 voters who pledged to refuse bribes, sparked the interest of Brazilians who then arranged for the Taiwanese to visit Brazil before a national election. And a Catholic woman from Croatia spoke of the 'deep experience of forgiveness' she had found with the help of a Hindu who had been caught in India's ethnic violence.

The impact of this great diversity of encounters can never be gauged. As Harold Saunders, former US Assistant Secretary of State, commented: 'Change does not begin in the government offices but in the human arena. The challenge is to take these transforming interactions where healing takes place out from a forum like Caux into the body politic.'

South Africans Sam Pono from Mamelodi West and Professor Willi Esterhuyse of Stellenbosch University describe their country 'crossing the threshold of hope'

Jamaica's Governor-General Sir Howard Cooke has brought over 70 Jamaicans to Caux

The Vice-Mayor of Tangshan , Mrs Yao Huixin, speaks for the first of the delegations from the Chinese Association for International Understanding

(*Right*) Msgr Mato Zovkic, the Roman Catholic Vicar-General of Sarajevo, talks with Israeli religious educator and peace activist Yehezkel Landau

Over the past decade Lebanese, often divided in their homeland, have met at Caux. 'These conferences have been a school of dialogue for us,' said a Druze judge

Sudanese, Somalis, Ethiopians, Eritreans talk of their work of reconciliation with delegates from Asia and America

... and enabling each person's part in peace-making

Anna Abdallah Msekwa, Tanzanian initiator of Creators of Peace: 'We all pretend that someone, somewhere is the stumbling block... Could that someone be myself? The individual is the prerequisite, a determining factor of peace.'

Four of the eight-member team from Creators of Peace who were in Beijing for the 1995 UN World Conference and NGO Forum on Women

Yukika Sohma, pioneer of a Japanese non-governmental organisation aiding refugees: 'None of us lacks the vision for peace. What we often lack is the first step in action, to start where we are.'

A s a Tanzanian Minister of State, Anna Abdallah Msekwa has seen many conferences on peace degenerate into contentious exchanges of political viewpoints. Her dissatisfaction sparked *Creators of Peace*, a network of people from many creeds and countries discovering their own peace-making potential. 'We should start initiating peace in the world from where we are, in our heart, home, work-place and community,' said Minister Abdallah, at the 1991 launching in Caux of this women's initiative.

Painful to listen to

Louise Diamond, conflict-resolution specialist with the US-based Institute for Multi-Track Diplomacy, watched the 680 women and men – representing 62 nationalities – and wondered what made this different.

She heard a Palestinian woman, agonised by her own recurring anger towards Israeli soldiers who killed her brother. And a founder of the Israeli 'Women in Black' telling of their persistent efforts to create dialogue not just with Palestinians but, on the other side, with extremists among their own people. Dr Diamond also met an Afrikaner journalist who, while visiting the homes of African women, had found it 'so painful to be quiet and listen to stories that you don't want to hear'; and her black compatriot who, after being in Caux in 1956, had returned to South Africa and mobilised 10,800 women in a movement 'to uplift the dignity of our people'.

The unique factor, concluded Dr Diamond, is 'the cumulative power of each one's truth, simply shared... and the commitment to live as one in and with the divine plan which opens the door to reconciliation and right relationships'.

'What seemed difficult became possible in the light of the experiences shared by others here,' said a Lebanese woman, illustrating the point. 'One thing is sure. I am no longer the same person. I am ready to change, to accept the other person and listen.'

Creators of Peace at its first session in Caux, 1991, with 680 women and men from 62 nations

A process of change at all levels of society

We are nearly at the end of this document and it would take many more pages to describe today's programs in Caux. Often they have developed from a suggestion by one individual. For example:

❏ From 1988, **scientists, industrialists and politicians** have gathered each year for a seminar on *The Preservation of Creation* initiated by Cardinal Franz König of Vienna. Listing 'seven deadly threats' facing mankind – pollution of the atmosphere, oceans and water resources, loss of soil fertility, de-forestation, endemic unemployment, the population explosion and spiritual pollution – they declare that 'ecological problems facing the world are so vast that an inter-disciplinary' approach is essential.

❏ British publisher William Porter, revisiting Caux in 1990, realised that he had been so focussed on his and his company's success that he had paid scant attention to how **the communications industry** could become not just the biggest but the most responsible in the world. With colleagues from different branches of the media, he launched at Caux in 1991 a series of *International Communications Forums* for media professionals. ICF Forums and seminars have been held in cities as far apart as Chicago, New Delhi and Nizhni Novgorod.

❏ From a series of Caux gatherings **educators** from kindergarten to university level have produced courses on 'education for character and world responsibility' and launched a bimonthly journal for fellow teachers.

❏ **Dutch families** have convened an annual New Year gathering for parents and children about the trends impacting family life. Over Christmas the mixture of winter sports and inter-generational dialogue has proved very popular.

❏ Winter has also given **farmers** from the First and Third Worlds a chance to leave their fields and work together on how to enlarge their responsibility for land-use planning, the environment, development and the relationship between today's society and its agriculture.

❏ **Health professionals** have seized the chance to bring together such extremes of their profession as Third World community health workers, research scientists and ordinary patients to examine the moral and spiritual issues confronting them.

At the Preservation of Creation dialogue, Massachusetts Institute of Technology physicist Victor Weisskopf, who headed Europe's CERN project, relaxes with American inventors Stanford and Iris Ovshinsky, who together have pioneered and developed the nickel metal hydride battery and solar energy systems

What could Caux contribute to the world of tomorrow?

We asked this question of a range of thinkers.
Their replies...

Inner development for outward responsibilities

Ahunna Eziakonwa, Lagos, post-graduate student of International Affairs, New York

In this era of profound cultural transition, institutions such as the UN groan under the weight of their global responsibilities. The international community faces the challenge of replacing the culture of violence and disharmony with one of peace and spiritual renewal.

Caux can complement the efforts already being made and add new dimensions to them. In 50 years of experimentation, through spiritual discipline and devotion to diversity, Caux has brought people together to search for a common goal rather than dwell on divisive elements. It has fostered inner development for outward responsibilities and provided the environment to conceive and develop ideas that contribute to change.

Caux helps establish a soul-centred life, inviting beauty, love, simplicity and culture into lives that are often too busy with activities, into imaginations filled with negative images, relationships cluttered with misunderstandings and a future burdened with complexities. Caux can continue to be the oasis where we can all be relieved of our plenty, acknowledge our need for one another, and become willing to be spiritually enriched for the good of all.

Ahunna Eziakonwa

A new task for a new world

**Masahide Shibusawa,
Director-CEO,
Tokyo Jogakkan School for Women**

During the years after World War II, when the world was repeatedly threatened to its core by the global confrontation of ideology, Moral Re-Armament proved itself to be remarkably effective in reconciling nations who were at each other's throats, or defusing crises to avoid their brutal outcome at the last moment.

By way of awakening moral and spiritual forces which were thus far dormant in men and women at critical moments of history, it produced unexpected and often miraculous results, proving time and again that man's soul and spirit, if and when properly led, could become a catalyst for inspired unity not only in the lives of individuals but in the fate of nations. Unfortunately, however, the magnitude of such achievements and their implications were not always acknowledged as such by the political establishment of the day, or recorded properly in the annals of the world. This was due in part to the bias of pervasive materialism of the modern world, communist and non-communist alike, and partly due to the pattern of its own activity which, stemming largely from personal experience rather than institutional endeavour, was considered incompatible with secular political evaluation.

The world, however, has changed. With the demise of the Cold War, it is openly in search of a fresh new approach, secular and spiritual. It is hoped that Moral Re-Armament would regenerate its vigour and, refining its time-tested modus operandi, address itself with the world which, though mercifully saved from the peril of ideological warfare, is yet fraught with renewed danger of religious and ethnic divide, to say nothing of the ever-worsening hazards of poverty and the environment.

M. Shibusawa

A standing invitation to build community

Joseph V Montville, Senior Associate at the Center for Strategic and International Studies, Washington, DC

In 1973 the psychoanalyst Leo Rangell, spurred by official American deception over the Vietnam War and the Watergate scandal, wrote of the 'lack of credibility, sincerity and authenticity from the highest offices in the land to the base of the population pyramid'. The 'compromise of integrity' he described has been more the worldwide rule than the exception throughout history. And the flaws have been not only in politicians but in the societies that produced them, the 'base of the pyramid'.

Caux has been one of the rare magical places where the human aspiration to integrity and community has been allowed to flourish. There, self-seeking and sectarian defensiveness have been subordinated to a much broader vision of the universal community of souls. Year after year Caux serves as a model for multicultural social integrity.

But Caux has made an even more important contribution to our potential for community by encouraging standards of political leadership which elude even the oldest democracies. For all its current problems the European Union remains the system to which all nations aspire in the post-Cold War era. The genius of Jean Monnet, and the moral commitment of Robert Schuman and Konrad Adenauer, in conceiving of community in a Europe savaged by ethnic conflict is one of the greatest achievements in human history.

These political leaders, of rare moral strength and integrity, found that Caux shared and nourished their vision. But non-political leaders also came to Caux representing commerce, labor, industry, journalism, arts and religion to play their critical role in building the practical aspects of multicultural community. If there were gaps in political leadership, the non-politicians did not hesitate to show the way.

The model of European Union nurtured at Caux is a standing invitation to build community between Islam, the West and Hindu India; to accelerate reconciliation between the Latin Church and Orthodoxy; to welcome Russia generously into Europe and help her bridge the civilizations of Central Asia and Europe. Caux stands always at the service of brotherhood and sisterhood amongst Africans and between them and the rest of the world; and is ready to help European descendants in the Americas build genuine community with first nations and the descendants of Africans.

Caux is a precious resource for humankind.

Jo V Montville

Meeting or missing the challenges of human history

Pierre Spoerri, journalist and author, Zürich

Great expertise and resources are employed in staying ahead of the game technologically and in marketing. But very few people even try to anticipate the movement of human history and influence it positively. Caux has given us a glimpse of that possibility.

But only a glimpse. In the immediate post-World War II years Frank Buchman and those working with him were far ahead of the thinking of their time. At a moment when practically nobody was ready to speak to Germans and to see any role for Germany in Europe, the first Germans were already in Caux, ready for a dialogue with their former enemies. In helping the Japanese to develop their democracy and to re-establish links with their Pacific neighbours, the group working in Caux was also far 'ahead of the game'. The same was true for some chapters of the history of decolonisation in Asia and Africa.

Like our governments, too many of us have found ourselves reacting too late to events. Caux, at its best, has been a stimulating forum for those actively involved in the fields which may well determine the future of humanity – fields like the constructive dialogue between cultures and religions; the healing of wounds inflicted by history; the challenge of the new information society.

But even that cannot ensure being 'ahead of the game'. Fundamentally, all any of us can do is daily make ourselves available to God, and let Him take us to the cutting edge of His transforming power in our lives and our societies. Then sometimes we are privileged to know that – often in spite of ourselves – we have played some part in preparing, with others, a new step forward for humanity. Caux's future is as a place where anyone or any group can contribute to that search.

Pierre Spoerri

Tackling the causes of nationalism and racialism

Rajmohan Gandhi, Centre for Policy Research, New Delhi, journalist and biographer of his grandfather, Mahatma Gandhi

Individualism is the common foe against whom all of us should pit our energies. 'I'll do what I want, when I want and the way I want' seems common to clashes at home, in the workplace and on the street, between ethnic and national groups – and even between research scientists seeking answers to killer diseases.

This foe is the deadlier for wearing the clothes of priceless allies such as individuality, identity and freedom. It is the fuel that keeps racialism and nationalism going, as well as the barbed wire that shuts out help and helpers. Complacent individualists make a soil fertile for terrorism; ambitious individualists, irrigating that soil with the blood of innocents, grow thorn trees of power. Translated as 'our national interest is not involved', individualism prevents a well-informed world from acting against inhumanities in 'remote' parts – sometimes as remote as a hundred kilometres away.

Caux has mediated to the world both a spirit and a fellowship – a spirit of listening (to the other person, the other race, the other nation, as well as to the inner voice, or as some may put it, to the whispers of God) and a fellowship of listeners alive to the pride and pain of others.

Exercises aimed at conflict-resolution are more common today than some years ago. Yet Caux remains unique. This listening to both the 'adversary' and the inner voice distinguishes its process from other dialogues. Caux stands out in its ability to let the world enter its heart. I see this as its special calling in the years ahead.

Rajmohan Gandhi

A breath of life for families

Nathalie Chavanne, mother of two, Versailles

The stress of modern life has overwhelmed today's families. We have stopped having time for each other. So we produce adults with hang ups or wounded personalities. But in Caux we learn that our hurts, our frustrations and our conflicts can also be the chinks through which a new spirit can enter our lives. My husband Frédéric and I have experienced this and found a new quality of dialogue.

A French journalist headed his report about Caux, 'The citadel of silence'. He highlighted one of its main purposes – to offer the environment and atmosphere where men and women, free from the pressure and bustle of their everyday life, can discover the transforming power of silence and of listening to the voice within. Could this breath of new life revive many families in an age when the whole system of traditional values has collapsed? Our homes are meant to be places where we learn what happiness is all about.

N. Chavanne